The Fearful Mind

THE FEARFUL MIND
A Psychological Portrait of Our Most Misunderstood Emotion

ALBY ELIAS

Essex, Connecticut

Prometheus Books
An imprint of The Globe Pequot Publishing Group, Inc.
64 South Main Street
Essex, CT 06426
www.globepequot.com

Copyright © 2025 by Alby Elias

All rights reserved. No part of this book may be reproduced in any form or by any electronic or mechanical means, including information storage and retrieval systems, without written permission from the publisher, except by a reviewer who may quote passages in a review.

British Library Cataloguing in Publication Information available

Library of Congress Cataloging-in-Publication Data available

ISBN 978-1-63388-936-1 (paperback)
ISBN 978-1-63388-937-8 (ebook)

∞™ The paper used in this publication meets the minimum requirements of American National Standard for Information Sciences—Permanence of Paper for Printed Library Materials, ANSI/NISO Z39.48-1992.

Dedicated to Dr. K. I. Koshy, a mathematician who proved that life is the most pleasant equation.

Contents

Foreword ix
Preface xi
Disclaimer xv

Chapter 1: Introduction 1
Chapter 2: The Origin and Development of Fear 13
Chapter 3: Unfriendly Anxiety 32
Chapter 4: Neurobiology of Fear 40
Chapter 5: Psychological Theories and Philosophy of Fear 47
Chapter 6: Fear: The Primary Psychological Force 60
Chapter 7: Benefits of Anxiety 68
Chapter 8: Role of Fear in Human Life and in Civil Society:
    Consequences of Fearlessness 82
Chapter 9: Optimal Anxiety 98
Chapter 10: Conclusions 107

Notes 111

Foreword

ANXIETY, HOWEVER NAMED, HAS LONG BEEN NOTED TO BE BOTH A PART of human existence and a potential cause of misery if uncontrolled. From ancient times, descriptions of racing thoughts, physical distress, and an impending sense of doom so typical of anxiety are clear. Descriptions of what we would now consider subtypes of anxiety, such as panic attacks, obsessive-compulsive disorder, and post-traumatic stress disorder, are equally easy to find. But many of these older descriptions failed to discriminate between what may be seen as pathological and what is normal.

The development of psychotherapeutic treatments including psychoanalysis in the first half of the twentieth century appeared to suggest that all anxiety was pathological and potentially reflective of deep-seated conflicts most likely rising from early life and requiring deciphering. Some years later, seminal work demonstrated that anxiety may not, in fact, always impair human performance and in certain circumstances may be beneficial to function. The evolution of diagnostic systems, such as the American Psychiatric Association's Diagnostic and Statistical Manuals in all of their versions have attempted to reinforce this by adding the presence of functional impairment to the definition of anxiety disorders, by default acknowledging that not all anxiety is worthy of a clinical diagnosis. It is of note that this not-perfectly-definable cutoff has not rendered anxiety rare. In the large-scale whole-population surveys conducted mainly in Western countries since the 1970s, anxiety disorders are increasingly seen as the most common mental health conditions, with the often-missed social anxiety disorder potentially being the most common.

Within broader popular culture, however, it appears that there is an increasing trend in some quarters to expect an anxiety-free life. The

Foreword

emphasis on stress and its role in our life and health and the ever-popular discussions about the busyness of modern life seem to place anxiety in a different frame of expectation. It is thus a timely undertaking to look again at what anxiety is, where it comes from, and when and where it is really a problem. Only then will we be best placed to know what we must do to reduce the crippling impact it can have for some, not the least by knowing how to direct our stretched mental health services most effectively. This volume represents a real opportunity to thoughtfully dive into these questions, problems that ultimately are relevant to us all.

Malcolm Hopwood
Professor of Psychiatry
The University of Melbourne
October 25, 2023

Preface

Fear is a paradox; it is perhaps the most undesirable emotion but the most wanted one for our survival. It is akin to pain. Fear and pain remind us of our imperfect evolution. We now have to live with anxiety. The anxiety literature has consistently shown that avoidance of anxiety makes it strong, and by facing it, we can soften it to a manageable level.

Sigmund Freud's remark that social anxiety is the root cause of conscience sparked my interest in writing this book. Since my exposure to psychiatry, I have seen the devastating effects of morbid anxiety at a staggering level; a panic attack is one of the worst human experiences. Extreme anxiety can be deadly.

Although excess anxiety is detrimental, moderate anxiety is normal and functional. Over time, I have learned that a certain degree of stress, particularly intermittent stress, is adaptive. Extremes destroy balance; in moderation, stress is healthy. It stimulates physiological and psychological adaptive response systems, increasing survival fitness.

This book aims to provide a detailed account of how fear and anxiety benefit our existence and daily lives. My central argument is that optimal anxiety motivates us to act creatively and safely, and the absence of it can lead to untoward consequences for both individuals and society. In attempting to present these views, I have relied on empirical evidence derived from systematic studies. These studies generated a wealth of knowledge about fear and anxiety. However, I must admit that, unlike natural sciences, psychological and social sciences are limited by a dearth of precise and objective data. Wherever relevant and possible, I have acknowledged these limitations and incorporated them into discussions.

After the first introductory chapter, an account of the origin and development of fear and anxiety is provided. To create a balance, negative aspects of fear and anxiety, although universally known, are illustrated. This is followed by the neurobiology of fear reactions. Psychological theories of anxiety, along with philosophical aspects, are presented in the next chapter. I have dedicated one chapter to demonstrating how powerful fear is and describing its dominance among emotions. If fear is strong, it overrides all other emotions; if love and happiness appear to operate freely, then the inference is that fear has retracted temporarily, or there is deficient fear, if not wholly absent. In the subsequent chapters, the book discusses the benefits of anxiety and the consequences of fearlessness in civilian life. Optimal anxiety, while a theoretical construct and hard to define, is described as a conceptual framework.

I have also synthesized the materials to form my proposals and opinions. They are my views, not necessarily of organizations, professions, or communities I am a part of. I conclude the book with a note on anxiety's unique aspect: its unpleasant nature is its survival value. These features of anxiety shake our customary notion—"abominable things are always to be abhorred"—and raise a fundamental question about human existence: A good journey seems to be tough, riddled with thorns, not only roses.

Preparation for this book took years. Perhaps my own anxiety forced me to make it comprehensive and accurate, but this can never be perfect. I am tremendously grateful to the publisher, Prometheus Books. Jonathan Kurtz, the executive editor, provided insightful and encouraging comments throughout its preparation. I also thank Felicity Tucker and Sean Sabo for copyediting and production.

Let me express my sincere thanks to Professor Malcolm Hopwood for kindly writing a foreword. During his busy hours as a professorial fellow in psychiatry, Mal was always supportive during my PhD career.

Family can be a source of anxiety in some instances, but it can also soothe anxiety at other times. On this occasion, I express my deep gratitude to my parents and brother, who brought me up to this level through their hardship, my wife Minu, and my children Anna and Mia for tolerating me with love and support while writing this book. I cannot thank my friend Sreekuttan enough for the greatest contribution to my life. He still reminds me that to save one's life from drowning, one has to conquer fear and thus be extraordinarily brave.

Notably, a good part of my learning was from my teachers and colleagues. I thank all of them, from whom I borrowed many ideas included

Preface

in this book. The vibrant and green campus of Thrissur Medical College, where I completed my medicine training, molded my career. Further to this, my psychiatry training at the National Institute of Mental Health and Neuro Sciences (NIMHANS) was critical in developing my understanding of anxiety. Vast resources in the libraries of these institutions, infused with a sense of tranquility, provided a fertile soil to learn.

I am thankful to my patients, who have been great teachers; their stories made my understanding of anxiety complex and rich. They were great sources of insight into the phenomenology of anxiety.

A.E.
Melbourne
February 26, 2025

Disclaimer

THE AUTHOR ATTEMPTED TO PRESENT EVIDENCE-BASED KNOWLEDGE derived from various studies. While a part of the book consists of such empirical knowledge, other parts contain the author's personal views and interpretation of findings in the literature. No part of the book is meant to represent treatment recommendations for anxiety or views of professional organizations.

Chapter One

Introduction

If a drug were found that abolished all anxiety for all time it could be as harmful as a drug that induced anxiety of crippling degree.
—Isaac Marks & Randolf Nesse[1]

Test anxiety is common. Excess anxiety is debilitative. There is a folklore that survived in medical schools about a medical student who was severely anxious. Although an otherwise brilliant student, he was reluctant to take examinations for fear of failure. One day, one of his close friends gave him an idea shortly before the following examination. The friend advised him to take antianxiety medication. It was seemingly an appealing suggestion, and the student, who was trembling with test anxiety, took the medication promptly. In a few hours, his trembling vanished. He was still anxious and unwilling to attend the examination, which was only two days away. He took the next dose. Soon, he felt confident to take the examination, and not long after, he decided to take it. After the third dose, he appeared pleasant; his friends were shocked to see the relaxed man trembling hitherto. The day before the examination, he proclaimed that the examination would be so easy for him that he did not have to prepare anymore. After a couple of hours, he wondered what examination it was. He did not feel a need for it. He did not care. The examination was inconsequential for him. He decided not to take the examination, but this time for a different reason—he was fearless and did not bother about the consequences of not taking the examination. His friends tried to convince him about the repercussions of not attending the examination but in vain. A lack of fear of consequences takes us to discuss the consequences of fearlessness.

Fear and anxiety are regarded as misfortunes in life. Arguably, liberation from fear brings tremendous potential for humans. One can be in full swing. Fear pulls us back. Are we at a loss each time we turn back because of fear? Fear leads to avoidance, and opportunities die. Pounding heart, tense trembling muscles, sweating, "butterflies in the stomach," and a sense of impending doom—the accompaniments of heebie-jeebies—are among the most uncomfortable feelings. Ever since the dawn of humanity, fear has been the most feared emotion. Anxiety was described in the writings of Hippocrates—notes about a young man terrified of flute music.[2]

History is replete with accounts that depict reason as noble, divine, and humane and passion as primitive and inferior, a disruptive force intruding into reason.[3]* Solomon observes that the wisdom of reason against treachery and temptations of passion characterizes Western philosophy. Anxiety is treated as inferior because it arises from imagined danger, implying that it is a creation of an irrational man, not a product of reality.[†] So, a stigmatizing figure of speech follows: "It is all in the head." Remarks made by Zeno of Citium are noteworthy in this context. Men refuse ill acts because of two reasons. When an action is declined according to reason, it is called caution; if unreasonable, it is called fear. Wise men do not suffer from fear. Also, passion is irrational and harmful.

Conscious feeling of fear infiltrates many spheres of our lives and influences daily affairs and decisions. Security systems installed in our homes, screening that we undergo at the airports, medications we take, and healthy lifestyles that we practice are influenced by fear. In this way, fear defines our lives and imparts an identity, a value, and a reminder that

---

* In *Faust*, Mephistopheles says: "Him a mere glimmer of the light of heaven;
  He calls it Reason…"
  Aristotle says, "Reason, more than anything else is man."
  In "An Essay on Man," Alexander Pope remarks: "What reason weave
  By passion is undone."

† Adam Smith says, "Fear is a passion derived altogether from the imagination, which represents … not what we really feel, but what we may hereafter possibly suffer." Smith, A. (1982/1759). *The Theory of Moral Sentiments*. Indianapolis, IN: Liberty Classics.

INTRODUCTION

life and its affairs are precious. Fear has economic and political dimensions. It was sometimes fear which was utilized in marketing strategies and business. Fear of pesticides prompts people to buy organic foods. Numerous pharmaceutical products are sold in the context of fear of ailments. People take various insurances for fear of catastrophic outcomes. In the modern world, it is hard to find things which are not insured.

Medical evidence suggests that regular use of sunscreen is associated with a reduced risk of skin cancer.[4] However, people may not buy sunscreen based on knowledge alone. On the other hand, if advertising campaigns depict skin cancers as a prominent theme, then the attitude toward purchasing sunscreen products may change because of fear appeals. If car insurance is advertised showing road accidents or legal battles after a crash, such an advertisement may have an additional impact on purchasing the insurance. Fear appeals work under certain conditions.[5] During political election campaigns, candidates may threaten society and induce fear with opponents' policies—for example, abolishing welfare funds or dangerous foreign policies. Fear pervades our society and forms a fear culture.*

Humans are the most intelligent animals; the putative mechanism behind our intelligence is a vast neuronal network. With a vast network, its structure and functions have become hugely diverse. The neuronal network thus brings disproportionate suffering from emotional disturbances.[6] Our brain, the body itself, has evolved imperfectly, and therefore we carry unhealthy characteristics. When we evolved, we could stand, but varicose veins and low-back pain are the prices we pay for our erect posture.[7] Our neuronal connections bestowed upon us not only desirable emotions such as happiness and love but also unpleasant emotions like anger and fear. Our minds evolved in mindless nature. Evolution does not assume any purpose and is therefore known as non-teleological; it just happens. Eyes are not made for us to see; we see because our eyes evolved. Fear evolved and has been preserved across species because it benefits reproductive survival. Evolution comes with a package. Fear is a part of it. Reacting to

---

* The manifestations of fear and anxiety are similar or at least overlapping, but they are conceptually and biologically different. Although these terms are used interchangeably throughout, anxiety is the essential subject of this book.

an unreal or imagined threat—for instance, a gunshot which is actually a firework—can be extremely unpleasant but not as dangerous as the other way—failing to fly in response to the threat of gun violence, thinking that it could be fireworks. We were born in a biological system with this imperfect characteristic. Our brain is wired to fly first and think second.

The modern view of emotions embraces advancements in science, particularly neurobiology, and entails a comprehensive understanding. *Emotions* are feelings experienced and expressed with physiological (bodily manifestations such as tremble), cognitive (thinking), and behavioral (actions) components. Emotions are the value system of the mind in that they are motivational, evaluative, and evocative, creating a sense of acting. Motivation refers to "forces acting either on or within a person to initiate behavior."*(For a detailed review of motivation, see chapter 5.) Fear has all aspects of emotions and is thus considered the prototype emotion. The neurobiology of fear is elucidated, albeit far from perfection. Anxiety was the central nucleus on which several psychological theories have been organized, and discourses and debates in psychoanalysis converge.

The word fear came from the old English word "faer," which meant sudden calamity; anxiety has multiple origins, two of which are noteworthy here: the Latin verb *ango*, meaning constriction, and a related word *angustus*, which means narrow.[8] These words have produced the modern German word *angst*. Fear has three dimensions: (a) autonomous arousal signals, such as sweating and palpitation; (b) muscular-behavioral, including trembling and motor movements like flight or approaching reactions; and (c) cognitive, consisting of conscious evaluation of the unpleasant feeling of fear. Fear and life are inextricable. *Fear* is universal; everyone will experience jitters regardless of age, gender, ethnicity, or culture. Initially described by Erasmus Darwin, birth trauma may cause fear.† Earlier, Sigmund Freud and, later, Otto Rank illustrated primal anxiety, which starts with the separation of a fetus from the uterus.[9]

---

* *Encyclopædia Britannica*. "Motivation." The word is derived from the Latin term *motivus*, meaning a "moving cause."
† Erasmus Darwin noted that one of the first influential sensations could be pressure on the precordium during birth signaling a lack of respiration. This is accompanied by a transition from 98-degree temperature to a cold atmosphere. It is argued that birth trauma and fear develop from these experiences.

INTRODUCTION

While birth anxiety is debatable, death anxiety is omnipresent. The awareness of the finitude of life, discontinuity of identity, and annihilation of existence generate fear. Fear of death and dying can sometimes take the form of thanatophobia. Between birth and death, the ebb and flow of fear rocks the conscious life and incessantly operates in the unconsciousness. Like banks accompanying a river from formation to destination, fear starts with the birth of man and dies with his death.

Varying Concepts of Fear

There is no unitary concept of fear or anxiety. For some, fear is a feeling state induced by danger. Some others consider it a set of physiological and behavioral reactions to the perception of danger. The common physiological reactions are a pounding heart, trembling, tense muscles, and sweating; the typical behavioral response to fear is avoidance of the fear-provoking situation or object. In the literature on fear, the term "danger" means any stimulus, object, or situation that can harm the organism. For Darwin, fear was a state of mind that was inherited from animals.* Panksepp described fear as an aversive state of mind.[10]† Other researchers view fear as a brain phenomenon mediating behaviors that avoid dangers due to threat perception.[11] Karen Horney described fear as a proportionate reaction to real danger. A phobia is a fear out of proportion. Psychologists, psychiatrists, philosophers, and laypeople use the word "anxiety" to connote a broad spectrum of meanings and experiences, all of which are difficult to group under a common umbrella.

Fear vs. Anxiety

A consensual understanding of fear is an unpleasant emotion elicited by danger with corresponding thoughts (cognitive), bodily signs

---

* Darwin remarks: "Some of the signs may be accounted for through the principles of habit, association, and inheritance, —such as the wide opening of the mouth and eyes, with upraised eyebrows, so as to see as quickly as possible all around us, and to hear distinctly whatever sound may reach our ears." Darwin C. (1872). *The Expression of the Emotions in Man and Animals*. Chicago: University of Chicago Press.

† Panksepp argues that fear is an old and primary emotion in that there is no need to learn it. It has been preserved during evolution. It can remain without cortical brain. See Panksepp J. (1998). *Affective Neuroscience*. New York: Oxford University Press.

(physiological), and actions (behavior). In the absence of a definite threat and the presence of an imagined and uncertain danger, the same set of phenomena constitutes anxiety. However, they are, in fact, two different phenomena.[12] Fear is a phasic response to a specific real threat and is ephemeral, whereas anxiety is enduring and may involve more than one type of anticipated threat. The brain regions that are responsible for fear and anxiety are different.[13] (See the remaining chapters for more information.) Fear is an immediate response to a proximal threat with an abrupt and conscious reaction. However, anxiety can be a gradual response to a distal and nebulous, often imagined danger with subtle manifestations or sometimes even unconscious implications. Some types of fear are inborn (see chapter 2 for a detailed account), and others develop instantaneously to new real threats. If a real threat (e.g., fire, electric shock) repeatedly and invariably follows a neutral object, then a presentation of the neutral object leads to anticipation of the same real threat and subsequent fear reaction even in the absence of the real threat. This learned fear reaction to an anticipated threat is anxiety.

Stress is yet another commonly used term. There is no unanimously agreed definition of stress. Broadly, stress refers to a condition that challenges the organism's homeostasis (or stability), requiring a response from the organism.[14] Another view is that stress denotes conditions where demands on the organisms exceed their natural regulatory capacity.[15]

Even though anxiety is a set of fear reactions arising from imagined danger rather than the presence of a well-defined real danger, morbid anxiety can be a storm in the head, so overwhelming that ignorance of the future is bliss. Although anxiety arises from the imagined future danger, its roots lie in past experiences that signified a threat to one's existence, well-being, or reputation. Therefore, anxiety is contingent on the past frightening experience and its memories that are woven into the imagination of the future. How did humans develop the ability to imagine? Giambattista Vico proposes that the ability to imagine occurred when the terror of the unknown forced humans to make sense of what terrified them—nothing is more dreadful than the unknown. Imagination is the best tool to deal with uncertainty as it brings some answers regardless of whether they are accurate. The skill of perception played a pivotal role in this process.[16] Thunder, for instance, aroused creative imagination in everyone. It was a common threat, and fear of such universal threats, Vico argues, paved the way for civilizations.[17] So, for the primitive man, terror led to the imagination.

It is not uncommon to see anxiety that is not attached to a specific object or situation. People often describe a sense of restlessness, a feeling of tense muscles, and difficulty concentrating without conscious recognition of a source of anxiety. They experience anxiety symptoms, the psychological feeling of being unpleasant, physiological features such as palpitation, and the mental component of an ominous future. They are, however, unable to pinpoint the source of their anxiety. Such anxiety with no specific content is known as free-floating or unattached anxiety.* It is sometimes a feature of generalized anxiety disorder or the early stages of psychosis.[18]

Crocq gives an account of panophobia and observes that, according to the historian of psychiatry German E. Berrios, Pitres and Regis gave the best description of panophobia, where a person is anxious about everything.[19,20] However, the content of anxiety randomly shifts from one situation to another, only transiently attached to specific content. Defensive reactions to threats are essentially the same in women and men except for yelling, screaming, or calling for help, which was frequent in women in controlled experimental settings.[21]

Hateful Fear

Fear elicits fight-or-flight reactions and alerts and prepares the organism against situations and objects of potential danger. Fear can, however, persist even when threatening objects no longer exist. It can also become generalized to nonthreatening objects or situations. It has tremendous potential to be contagious and hence to develop into various forms following initial occurrence. In this way, fear grows to new landscapes where it is unnecessary. Therefore, when fear builds up unnecessarily without threats, it becomes the most unwanted experience, a powerful and painful

---

* The World Health Organization's *International Classification of Diseases* 11th edition describes "General apprehensiveness that is not restricted to any particular environmental circumstance" as one of the features of generalized anxiety disorder.

human predicament. When anxiety exceeds a level and grows to the extent of causing disturbances in one or several areas of life, it becomes a disorder. Anxiety disorders are among the most common psychiatric disorders in many societies.[22] Anxiety is, therefore, a hateful emotion resulting in profound human suffering. Fear of happiness and having or receiving compassion have been described, and both are related to a high degree of self-criticism and depressed mood.[23] Depression is related to the appraisal of the past, while anxiety is essentially linked to estimating the untoward future.

Fallacies of Fear

According to the National Safety Council, the probability of road fatality is higher than that of an air crash. However, people are intensely anxious while flying, especially when a bumpy ride shakes the tray table. When statistics speak of excellent safety records in aviation, we do not find a reason for this "panic" other than man's inherent fear of heights. Anxiety does not follow the language of logic. There is an apparent predisposition for anxiety in humans; it comes out of the blue, on occasions instantaneously, allowing no prospect for reasoning. Fear is a fallacy—a creation of instincts and interpretations—but logic cannot eliminate it. For instance, we have every reason to be reassured to cross underwater tunnels, undergo open-heart surgery, or stand on the 100th floor of the Empire State Building. Still, one may quickly develop fear in such situations. Fear can sweep through the consciousness and eliminate all types of reasoning. This apparent senselessness of fear is consistent with the evolution of the different parts of the brain; the part of the brain that processes fear reaction was formed earlier than the regions involved in reasoning.[24] One of the brain principles is that the regions that evolved last will lose function first, and the regions that came first will go last.[25] Phylogenetically, the fear-processing brain region, known as the limbic system, came before the prefrontal cortex, which is involved in reasoning.

Moreover, connections from the limbic or emotional system to the cortical cognitive or reasoning system are more than the ones in the opposite direction.[26] In this sense, the higher brain need not be the mightier brain. Each region of the brain serves a distinct function.

Friendly and Useful Fear

Current literature about fear proliferated around anxiety disorders and their adverse impacts on human life. Proponents of mental well-being teach us how to get rid of fear. We should not fail to admit the devastating effects of morbid anxiety, but our vision will be selective and tubular if we confine ourselves to the negative aspects of fear. We are compelled to ask how fear has evolved and how unwanted and unreasonable anxiety has been preserved across species during evolution. One might argue that fear keeps us safe and alive. Fear is fundamental to human existence; it reminds us of our existence.

Evolutionary theories attempted to explain the adaptive and beneficial values of fear. This approach offered a simplistic explanation, however. Let us imagine, for a moment, that we are entirely deprived of fear. If men are otherwise capable of logically discerning the danger based on facts and reasoning, what would be the necessity of fear? Can we reasonably assume that our logical thinking takes precedence or dominance in analyzing threats? Can we relax, concluding that our logical thinking will find facts accurately and keep us safe? No. When fear disappears, other emotions, such as pleasure, love and instincts, drives, and excitement not dominant hitherto, will be the operative forces. The reason will give way to passion as it does to fear, and ethics will be subordinate to aesthetics. As Frijda observes, human beings are enslaved by their passion, one or another.[27] These statements do not appear as rhetoric or motherhood statements. They have biological, specifically neurological, underpinnings. If fear is absent, then another emotion will come in its place to engulf reason.

Fear, not a logical analysis of consequences, forms the primary force prohibiting the unshackled fulfillment of pleasure instincts. Therefore, reasoning alone is incompatible with survival. Fear, at least in certain instances, is necessary to combat positive emotions, the unconditional and unchecked fulfillment of which can threaten life. It ensures checks and balances within a system of maladaptive psychological defenses and external realities. Psychological defense mechanisms can be mature or immature and adaptive or maladaptive depending on the types, intensity, duration, and purposes they serve. For instance, a moderate, short-lasting denial of realities may give us momentary relief and prevent mental collapse.

Nonetheless, severe and sustained denial can be catastrophic. When bushfire spreads, people may deny that fire will encroach on their properties. During the spread of pandemics like COVID-19, people may deny it will not affect them. Passengers on a train keep their valuable items on the overhead rack, denying the risk of theft. While bringing peace of mind and reducing anxiety, these denials can eventually lead to devastating outcomes. Rationalization and minimization are other defense mechanisms people commonly employ to trivialize dangers and obtain peace of mind. These defenses can also be maladaptive and harmful.

We rarely see how fear operates and protects our day-to-day lives. The negative portrayal of fear is far from the universal truth. In *Hack Your Anxiety*, Alicia Clark intriguingly narrates how anxiety as a powerful motivating force can form a path to success.[28] Liddell remarked that anxiety accompanies intellectual activity as its shadow.[29] An optimal level of anxiety is associated with a high intelligence quotient (IQ).[30]

From an evolutionary point of view, fear originally developed against crude stimuli, like noises, heights, animals, and strangers. The threats in the modern world are different. The most significant dangers that threaten human survival, such as road traffic accidents and infectious and chronic diseases, do not belong to this group. Although fear evolved as an innate response to unrefined stimuli of the primitive age, humans learned fear reactions over time to the threats of modern life. Because of the fear of accidents, motorists control speed and become alert to road situations. People eat not only because they are hungry but also because they have the underlying fear of the consequences of starvation; they deliberately observe fasting as they fear illnesses resulting from excess food consumption. Men take medications due to the fear of worsening ill-health; produce offspring from the fear of discontinuity of species; wear clothes nicely because of the fear of social embarrassment; and follow protocols during construction and machinery operations because of the fear of a collapse or catastrophic industrial accidents.

Broadly, the approaches to fear and anxiety are the following: (1) neurobiological and psychological; (2) philosophical (which is largely existential); and (3) functional. Although an attempt has been made to describe all approaches, this book intends to stress the functionalism—the adaptive value of fear and anxiety. While conveying that fear reactions have enormous survival and adaptive value, this book does not intend to promulgate a view that fear is unconditionally good or desired. It does not take a position that fear is the all-inclusive factor determining the outcome of exposure to danger. In fact, fear is only one factor, but it is a critical one that is determinative in predicting survival success. Other factors, such as an individual's resources—memory, knowledge, past experiences, personality and resilience, and overall intellectual functions—play a crucial role in dealing with dangers and overcoming threats, both explicit and implicit. Therefore, the presence of fear alone without other psychological resources may not be adaptive, and such a fear reaction may even be counterproductive. Performance is a product of skills multiplied by arousal level. In this context, the concept of *eustress* captures manifold importance; it connotes positive reactions to danger, resilience, and resources to face threatening life experiences and often motivation.[31] *Eustress* literally means "good stress." The language of fear is the avoidance of perceived danger. At the same time, fear triggers action, and in that sense, it is a motivational force.

In the remaining parts of this book, we will see the critical role of fear in human life, particularly when danger is lurking. Fear and anxiety are tantamount and interchanging in this book, although they are conceptually and biologically distinct. Modern theories refer to "fears" in the plural form because a collection of closely related but distinct brain states about fear and different types of dangers associated with various neurological and behavioral responses have been identified. Despite these differences, fear and anxiety are brain phenomena originating in the intricate neuronal network. Such a root of fear and anxiety in neuroscience is presented at length in chapter 4. Before that, the general theories of fear development are described in chapter 2. Indeed, these theories are largely based on empirical research and readily observable phenomena.

Describing a complex psychological phenomenon in simplistic terms is a cumbersome task. Fear is understood imperfectly, and many aspects of it remain inexplicable. The strongest facet of fear, as far as human existence is concerned, is its necessity. It is a unique phenomenon because it is incumbent upon humans while portrayed as a negative emotion. The presence of fear in humans is a paradox, a mystery, the unyielding human predicament that resists an illuminative understanding. It puts a lid on human potential, but when all restrictive forces on humans vanish, fear evaporates, and when men become liberated from prohibitions, emptiness may ensue. In the absence of fear, man will deteriorate to a mass without his essence.

Although a good part of this book is based on findings from systematic studies, it is not an exclusive review of empirical data. Some of it corresponds to established facts, while others are postulates. Anxiety is double-edged and has neutral surfaces; we should not be blind to any dimensions. Anxiety can be bad, good, or neutral.

CHAPTER TWO

The Origin and Development of Fear

Anxiety is the very root of what it means to be human.
—DAVID BARLOW[1]

IT IS FUNDAMENTAL FOR LIVING ORGANISMS TO REACT TO HARMFUL stimuli. This reaction, typically a harm-avoidant behavior, is seen in almost all living creatures, including single-cell organisms. For example, when a bacterium avoids harmful chemicals with chemotactic movement, the avoidant reactions in larger organisms are mediated through a sophisticated nervous system.[2] While the conscious feeling accompanying such reactions may vary across species, fear is the typical experience in humans that is entwined with avoidant behavior.

The essence of anxiety is in the uncertainty of the future. Studies have demonstrated that the unpredictability of aversive events cause sustained fear.[3] In clinical practice, people suffering from unpredictable panic attacks become anxious about the next attack, and such anticipatory anxiety can be tormenting.[4] Essentially, fear is felt when the estimation of danger exceeds the sense of safety. The feeling of anxiety originates when the mind overestimates danger and underestimates safety with a shift of the danger-safety dyad toward the threat.

There are different types of fear, with differences mainly in the genesis, fear content, and the set of reactions that diverse kinds of fear induce. Different types of fears serve different adaptive purposes; for example, fear of heights may evoke freezing, fear of social threats may arouse submission, and if a tiger is attacking, then fear will serve the task of flight and avoidance.[5] The content of fear is defined by the situation or object represented in human consciousness, causing fear. When fear is such a ubiquitous phenomenon, its genesis is worth exploring. A person develops a fear of a place because of the direct experience of being assaulted there, witnessing another person being assaulted, or being instructed that an assault occurred there. The development of fear involves multiple mechanisms. This chapter deals with the origin and development of fear.

There is a debate on whether anxiety is inborn or learned. Specific anxious reactions (e.g., reaction to thunderous sound, fire, and height) are present from birth, suggesting that fear is an inborn quality, a primary emotional state that is irreducible and instinctive. Conversely, human beings develop a fear of other things as an acquired quality over a period. For instance, an infant does not show anxiety toward a man holding a revolver more than seeing a man holding a flower. Fear of such situations is acquired in the later part of life through learning from direct experience, social interactions, observations, and use of knowledge base. By the same token, certain other fearful reactions abate as children grow. Stranger anxiety and separation anxiety are classic examples. In the following sessions, we shall examine the literature on fear acquisition in depth.

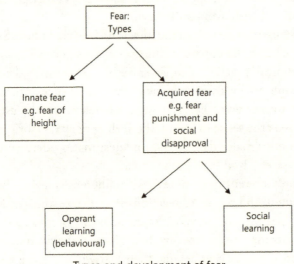

Types and development of fear

Inborn Fear

Long ago, William James argued that fear was an instinctive reaction to specific objects and situations and could not be reduced to any other psychological source. This implies that fear is a primary psychological phenomenon, not depending on other psychological developments. Studies of infants and children provided an engrossing account of the inborn nature of fear.* Certain types of fear are considered primary or inborn in that the fear-provoking stimuli have independent potential to induce fear. They cause fear without being associated with other fear-provoking stimuli. For a particular type of fear to be regarded as an inborn fear, it must meet specific criteria:

- It should have a plausible evolutionary basis.
- Associative learning is not required for the fear to develop.[6]
- Fear is found in primates, animals at the low levels of the evolutionary ladder, in whom it has an adaptive advantage.
- Substantial genetic contribution to the fear can be found.[7]

In a recent experiment, Hoehl et al. have proven that fears of snakes and spiders are inborn.[8] Pictures of snakes and spiders were shown to 48 infants, and their pupillary reaction was observed. Upon seeing snakes and spiders, the pupil's size increased, indicating increased adrenaline release, a biological reaction seen during the fear response. The pupil size change was not observed when infants saw pictures of fish or flowers. Although there is a limitation in infants' inability to articulate the emotion of fear, these findings imply fear because the reactions accompanying the adult experience of fear were seen in these infants.

Findings have accrued to suggest that fear of heights is an innate fear.[9] A follow-up study of children from the age of nine up to 18 years found that height phobia developed without prior falls or injury from heights, indicating that associative learning is not required for its

---

* Associative learning in this context refers to development of fear through a learned mechanism. This means fear of a new object or situation is learned by after the object or situation was associated with an original fear evoking object or situation.

development. Height fear is present in primates from the first day of life. Fear of heights was long thought to be present in infants based on the visual cliff paradigm.[10] Crawling infants crossed a visible surface of support but avoided crawling over a glass-covered precipice that constituted a meter-high drop-off. To ensure the safety of infants, the researchers made an illusory drop-off. It was concluded that infants feared heights, which was challenged in a recent experiment in which infants did not display signs of fear as they approached a cliff.[11] They instead explored possibilities of locomotion. It was later argued that the approach to a cliff and the actions were based on the perception of the environment and its relation to one's potential and resources. The environment gives some clues which indicate whether actions are affordable in terms of one's potential. For instance, jumping over a fence is within one's capability, but doing the same from the tenth floor of a building is not affordable. Clues about the environment—for example, height—are affordances, and actions are based on how a person interprets the affordances.[12] However, there is evidence that fear influences perceptual estimates of environmental affordances and subsequent actions; for instance, the depth may be overestimated if an individual is afraid.

Infants show reactions consistent with those of fear upon exposure to loud noises and loss of support.[13] In the final days of infancy, fears of strangers, strange places, and heights develop.[14] Fear of strangers is another type of inborn fear. Infants show distress upon seeing unfamiliar faces in contrast to familiar faces. Hebb argues that the origin of the fear of strangers lies in violation of expectancies, the discrepancy between the familiar and unfamiliar.[15] In another experiment, one group of chimpanzees was provided with normal visual experiences, including of other chimpanzees, while the other group was blindfolded. When exposed to the plaster replica of a chimpanzee's head, the visual exposure group that already saw normal chimpanzees reacted with fear, and the blindfolded group showed curiosity. Hebb inferred that the group that had visual exposure to other chimpanzees had already developed a mental schema of normal chimpanzees, and the sight of the familiar but incomplete figure—the head without a torso, hands, or limbs—evoked fear.[16]

The above type of fear response requires the maturational development of mental schema. A change in familiarity and habit can be confronting because such a change may involve disrupting brain representations of previous experiences and associated memories. After all, memories are produced by brain chemicals and circuits. Therefore, a departure from the existing neurobiological network evokes specific reactions, which may produce an unpleasant experience. Due to the lack of familiarity, strangeness may signify precariousness and produce a sense of unfamiliarity and unknown and, therefore, fear.

Valentine has pointed out inherent limitations in assessing fear in infancy.[17] We can only rely on signs similar to those displayed by adults when they experience fear. However, it is widely agreed that loud sounds produce specific signs different from pain cries or hunger cries. These signs are being startled, throwing up the arms, and the holding of breath. As Hebb proposes, the sudden noise and unexpected loss of support excite fear, not when the sound is gradually built up or when the drop is verbally prepared. Given their sudden and unexpected nature, these stimuli are psychologically unanalyzable. The rapidity with which the stimulus occurs does not allow enough time for psychological functions to process information. Such perceived powerlessness may be another theme behind the genesis of the sense of fear. In addition, as in the case of strangeness, the trigger of fear lies in the discrepancy or conflict between the pattern previously and frequently experienced by the subject and the sensory input perceived as novel and different from the preexisting cerebral process. This is the *conflict theory* of fear.[18] Jones proposes that unexpectedness is a common feature of several fear-provoking stimuli.[19] Likewise, fear of the dead and mutilated bodies arises from the unexpected, unfamiliar, and rapid perception, which can disrupt the previously existing organized cerebral process.

Attempts to reorganize the cerebral process result in coordinated actions that eventually lead to avoidance of the stimulus. The new cerebral organization may develop with repeated exposure to the unfamiliar stimulus, and fear will eventually be extinguished. However, if the stimulus is avoided, such a reorganization will fail to develop. Avoidance of fear-inducing stimuli eventually results in strengthening fear. This is, in fact, a reinforcement of fear and a perpetual process—the more the avoidance, the more robust the fear will be.

OTHER TYPES OF FEAR IN EARLY LIFE

Fear of being alone, animals, and darkness evolves later in life around the preschool years.[20] The underlying theme is a threat to existence. Children develop fears of supernatural phenomena, failure, criticism, and physical injury in school.[21] Fear of danger and death persists throughout life.[22] Fear of death develops as early as five years of age, but it is during early adulthood (20 years to 40) that it becomes prevalent.[23] Death anxiety peaks during middle adulthood (40 years to 60 years). Interestingly, death anxiety remains, then declines afterward. At age 13, fear of speaking in front of the class was the most common; by age 15, fear of talking to new people was also prevalent.[24]

Although fear is induced by certain stimuli early in life, this kind of fear is relatively short-lived. In a sample of eight- and nine-year-old children, Spence and McCathie showed that all types of fears faded over two years except the fear of death, danger, and injury.[25] Reduction in the original types of fear is striking in the early years of life. Qualities of stimuli are critical in determining fear reactions. High intensity, sudden onset, and proximity to the threatening stimulus may induce an extreme fear reaction, sometimes to freezing of the exposed organism. If the threatening stimulus is at a distance, fleeing instead of freezing could be the outcome. The types of fear or situations of fear change over the lifespan. Stanley Hall[26] gives an insightful account of how fear sometimes fits best with the past than the present: snakes and animals need not induce so much fear in the present civilized life, and the sound of thunder does not produce as much fear as it did in the early years.

Nevertheless, we must bear in mind that the rule of fear is not the rule of logic. The genesis of fear does not recognize the language of reason. Reasoning is a time-consuming process, and for men to increase the probability of survival from dangers, swiftness of response is the key. Fear fits with this purpose.

Acquired Fear and Mechanisms of Fear Acquisition

This type of fear requires the presence of other factors for its development. It does not develop *de novo*. The following theories explain the mechanisms of fear acquisition.

Behavioral Theories

The essential principle of acquired fear is that an object or situation that is initially neutral and not fear-provoking later develops fearful qualities after it is paired with an originally fear-provoking stimulus. This process is called conditioning. According to behavioral theories, fear is conditioned. We will see this soon with the help of a few examples.

The first is classical conditioning. The origin of fear lies in two mechanisms: memory of the traumatic experience, and anticipation of the same experience in the future. Therefore, in fear, the past and future are interwoven. In an animal experiment, rats in a cage were exposed to electric shock following the sound of a buzzer. This sequence was repeated several times. Initially, the rats felt pain and fear upon receiving an electric shock. Over repeated presentation of the buzzer and then electric shock, the buzzer alone acted as a warning, resulting in anxiety. The buzzer was originally a neutral sound, a stimulus that did not produce fear on its merit. After the electric shock sequentially followed the buzzer, it produced fear even when the electric shock did not follow. The buzzer has thus become a conditioned stimulus, and fear that develops following the buzzer has become a conditioned fear response.

Conditioning occurs not only to the explicit cue—the bell—but also to implied cues such as the cage or environments related to the explicit cue. Responses to these environments or contexts are also conditioned and are known as *contextual conditioning*.[27] Reactions to explicit cues are more definite and phasic than contextual cues, which are sustained and potential threats. The former reaction is like fear, and the latter enduring reaction is anxiety. Moreover, when the cues and subsequent electric shock occur unpredictably, the contextual conditioning—the anxiety—becomes intensified.

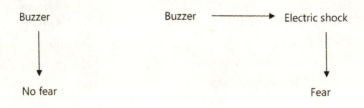

Figure 1. Originally buzzer does not produce fear.

Buzzer followed by electric shock produce fear.

Sequence repeated several times.

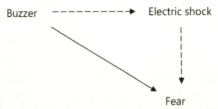

Buzzer produces fear without electric shock.

From the previous experiment, it is seen that stimuli (objects and situations) evoke fear through fear conditioning, a process in which a previously neutral stimulus (buzzer) turns into a conditioned stimulus (CS) through pairing with a primary fear-provoking unconditioned stimulus; in this instance, electric shock. This temporal and contiguous association acts as the seed for anxiety. In the case of a contiguously paired stimulus, the initially neutral stimulus becomes no more neutral; it is incorporated into the memory of an initially frightening stimulus. In a way, this is a learned mechanism that involves memory. This is conditioned learning. Upon exposure to the conditioned stimuli, the organism starts anticipating danger, and this anticipation leads to anxiety. The strength of anxiety depends on the number of repetitions of pairing and the strength of the frightening stimulus. Stimuli that bear some similarities with fear-inducing ones also can induce anxiety. Such stimuli are called secondary conditioned stimuli. Wolpe and Rachman proposed that any neutral object, originally not fear-provoking, may acquire the ability to evoke fear subsequently if it happens at about the time when other stimuli evoke fear.[28] This means there will be a generalization of fear reactions to stimuli similar to the original fear-provoking stimulus.

The best illustration of fear generalization is seen in combat soldiers. There have been vivid accounts of fearful and disturbed behaviors in soldiers.[29] Soldiers develop intense fear reactions long after a war when they are exposed to cues and reminders of their experience in the combat field. Such fear reactions may be induced by the sound of a helicopter, a crowd in civilian life, or watching a war documentary on television. This fear syndrome has been described as part of war neurosis (later known as post-traumatic stress disorder). This may be taken as a consequence of the generalization of fear stimuli from war zones to civilian life. In this manner, fear is a contagion as it spreads from the original stimulus to related situations and objects and thus becomes chronic and disabling morbidity. Affected individuals reexperience the trauma through intrusive memories, nightmares, and flashbacks, all accompanied by fear reactions.

Anticipation and imagination are unique to human beings.[30] Humans feel comfortable with a solid sense of self, time, and space. In a delirious state, there will be disorientation to time, space, and person. Lack of a well-defined sense of self with orientation to space and time can be uncomfortable and painful. This applies to uncertainty about the future. Grupe and Nitschke argue that the ability to use past experiences and current information to increase the odds of the desired outcome in the future and reduce the odds of adversity is present in humans.[31] This ability is proportional to the certainty of the future. Uncertainty diminishes the efficiency of our preparation for the future. Uncertainty is intolerable, and humans handle uncertainty by making assumptions and anticipations.

When anticipation involves a negative outcome, it leads to anxiety. Although the danger is not real, the anticipated or imagined danger induces anxiety. It is well known that overestimating danger and underestimating safety form the crux of anxiety. The mechanisms of operation of fear and anxiety are different. The biological and psychological mechanisms of the induction of fear differ from anxiety. Anxiety is, therefore, a response to the past through memory and the future through imagination. Recognition of the conditioned stimulus (initially not fear-provoking) requires memory, and anticipation requires imagination. Fear is thus a unique emotion that encompasses memory of past information and imagination.

The second behavioral theory is operant learning. After an animal is given an electric shock repeatedly, it is given an opportunity to press a bar that switches off the electric stimuli. In this instance, the behavior of pressing the bar is reinforced through a learning mechanism called operant learning. In the first experiment of buzzer and electric shock described earlier, Mowrer observed that the animal escaped upon hearing the buzzer, the warning.[32] This behavior is negatively reinforced in the sense that the reward for the behavior is avoidance of or escape from the electric shock. This behavior has become conditioned avoidance. This forms the basis of fundamental human behavior of fleeing from a frightening situation upon seeing warning signs and anticipation of danger. Mowrer argues that fear motivates human beings to react, and reducing fear, in turn, reinforces the escape behavior that brings a sense of relief or security.[33] Reducing fear is undoubtedly a pleasant experience that every organism would welcome, and therefore it will have a reinforcing effect on escape behavior. Nonetheless, it is fear that motivates escape behavior. The avoidant response eliminates fear only temporarily. In the long term, not only is that fear not eliminated by avoidance, but it is also that it is strengthened each time the warning is heard. When the fear is intensified, the escape behavior is also amplified, setting up a vicious circle. Each time the animal escapes painful stimuli, it escapes the fear-provoking situation, not the fear itself. Mowrer stated that anxiety is a learned response, occurring to signals premonitory of situations of injury or pain. Rachman argues that the best evidence for conditioning theory comes from animal studies in the laboratory and also limited data from human studies, but they broadly apply to fear from physical trauma.[34]

Social Learning Model

Social learning is a powerful way of acquiring a predisposition to certain mental states and habits.[35] When behavioral models expound on direct learning of fear, social learning theory deals with the indirect acquisition of fear through transmission across conspecifics through observation and instruction. Human beings have a unique ability to learn emotional expression in the conspecific through visual representation and language. Infants scan their environment. When an infant is exposed to a new environment and strangers, it looks at the mother to see her reaction. If she smiles, the infant will be reassured; if she is frightened, the infant will develop fear. When an individual observes an electric shock in another person, the observer develops fear merely through observation. This is observational fear learning. An individual may develop fear when verbal information is given that touching an electric wire will lead to electric shock but without direct observation. This is called instructed fear. During social learning, objects of observation are modeled. When children regularly watch anxious behaviors in parents, they eventually model these behaviors through a process called vicarious learning.[36]

Findings derived from experiments support the above hypothesis of fear acquisition by observation and instruction. These studies suggested that fear can develop not only after direct learning after the experience of an aversive stimulus but also by observing fear reaction in others and receiving an instruction that an aversive stimulus is imminent.[37] In an experiment, children were shown two stimuli, and they were alternatively followed by positive and fearful facial expressions by their mother.[38] When these stimuli were shown again after a short delay, the one followed by the fearful expression by their mother induced fear. Another experiment showed that subjects developed fear reactions after being instructed that they would receive a shock after a conditioned stimulus and were later exposed to the same conditioned stimulus.[39] Children experienced fear after storytelling; they reported fear and phobia after watching fearful parents.[40] Fear of spiders in mothers was associated with fear of spiders in their children.[41] This suggests that fear can develop after observation and verbal instruction.

Social learning plays a pivotal role in creating and maintaining human culture.[42] Exposure to social cues that signify a scared conspecific can induce a fear response, a phenomenon known as *fear contagion*. Development of fear may be impaired in the presence of a familiar reassuring conspecific through a mechanism called *fear immunization*.[43] Fear learned through social exposure may attenuate in the presence of a familiar reassuring conspecific, and this is *the social buffering of fear.*[44] If parents are overprotective and intrusive and overestimate dangers, children will learn that the world is unsafe. In a twin study, such a social learning effect was found to be independent of genetic influences.[45]

In contrast to popular belief, watching programs depicting frightening scenes on television was not associated with phobia.[46] Although 51.7 percent of patients with phobia reported exposure to frightening objects on television programs, there was no significant difference in exposure between subjects with phobia and those without phobia in television exposure. In the same vein, vicarious learning from motion pictures or print media was insignificant in acquiring fear.

THE EVOLUTIONARY ASPECT OF FEAR

> *Men during countless generations have endeavored to escape from their enemies or danger by headlong flight.*
> —CHARLES DARWIN[*]

In support of the evolutionary origin of fear, defensive reactions to threats are similar in humans and animals. Darwin's unerring fingers in an unexplored land of observation brought an edifice of knowledge. According to Darwin, fear is preceded by astonishment, and the reactions are the same: raised eyebrows and widely opened mouth and eye.[47] These changes help organisms see widely. Accompanying these changes, superficial muscles shiver during the fear reaction. A dreadful scream of terror can be heard at the height of fear. For Darwin, there was good reason to believe that these reactions made the animal appear terrible to its enemy. At other times, a frightened man may stand motionless and breathless or crouch down to escape the sight of predators. Traits and behaviors that offer reproductive advantages will undergo natural selection. The physiological and behavioral reactions that constitute fear are responses that increase the ability to deal with dangers and the odds of survival. When

---

[*] Charles Darwin, *The Expression of the Emotions in Man and Animals.*

a ferocious animal attacks, a flight reaction or avoidance helps survival. Social anxiety is adaptive when social disapproval prevails.[48] Marks describes such a reaction as akin to physiological phenomena such as sneezing and diarrhea that are meant to keep pathogens away.

Notably, fear reactions are universal, and they occur even in isolated areas where people have little contact with the rest of the world.[49] This observation suggests a link to a common origin of fear rather than cultural transmission of fear behavior and questions social learning theory as the only mechanism of fear development. Moreover, fear reactions are more or less the same across species, implying phylogenetic conservation of fear.*[50] This hypothesis is further supported by the fact that fear response circuits in the human brain and other mammalian brains share common areas.[51] The above findings point toward an evolutionary basis of the origin of fear.

Emotions that serve specific tasks survived through natural selection. Love is related to reciprocity, which has a survival advantage. Aggression is another example: It is a defense mechanism to help fight a threatening enemy of the same status. Emotions are products of countless incidences of trial and error resulting from myriads of accidental gene mutations. How does an orchestrated mechanism work in defense of humans? The answer is in the timescale. According to the existing data, living creatures and biological phenomena are the results of countless permutations and combinations tested in nature during the process of natural selection over billions of years.[52] How many things can occur during this period? This timescale should have allowed the emergence of combinations that could not survive and, later, their elimination and the selection of combinations that could adapt to the external world. Fear is not an exception; neither are humans. The answer to our reluctance to accept the natural formation of the current design of the living kingdom is our limited ability to comprehend the vastness of the above timescale.

A mixture of emotions serves multiple purposes. The presence of one threat implies the likelihood of others. Evaluation and social learning

---

* LeDoux argues that the fear response circuits and defense systems, rather than conscious feelings of fear, are common in animals and man. J. E. LeDoux, *The Emotional Brain: The Mysterious Underpinnings of Emotional Brain*, p. 130. London: Phoenix.

have a better chance of survival as they allow the organisms to adapt to the environment without many reflex reactions to varying dangers. The ability to solve variable and novel problems is critical to successful adaptation. Learning is helpful in the process of adaptation to diverse and variable challenges in long-lived species.

Marks and Nesse illustrate specific anxiety reactions that may have a survival advantage.[53] In heights, freezing from fear can prevent falls; public spaces mean being away from one's home and home to extraterritorial species, and public fear can be adaptive in avoiding danger from unknown species or attackers. The public fear may lead to cohesion within the group of known members and enhance social bonding. As seen in post-traumatic psychological reactions, increased arousal symptoms such as vigilance and avoidance help prevent reexposure to potential danger. Submissive behavior and shyness out of fear may promote acceptance.

The development of anxiety closely parallels the evolution of intelligence.[54] A study demonstrated a positive correlation between intelligence and worry within a group of patients with generalized anxiety disorder, although it was inversely correlated with worry in healthy controls.[55] It

Charles Darwin
WIKIMEDIA COMMONS

is noteworthy that the mean intelligence score was higher in the anxiety disorder group than in the control group.[56]

GENETIC AND DEVELOPMENTAL INFLUENCE

The Swedish data registry is well known for twin studies. Twins have a genetic similarity. A study of 2,490 Swedish twins between the ages of eight and 20 suggested the heritability of fear.[57] The twins received a questionnaire through the mail and rated the intensity of fear in various situations. Evidence suggests moderate heritability of specific phobia.[58] Although fear changes over time and with age, the identical twins rated fear similarly, whereas nonidentical twins did less. Such a similarity became less identical as the twins grew older, suggesting other factors influencing fear expression. The genetic basis of fear was well demonstrated in mice. Mice were exposed to frightening stimuli, and it was found that the fear reactions varied among mice; some showed little fear, some intense fear, and others exhibited moderate fear. Fearful mice were allowed to breed with each other, and the young generations showed the same fear pattern regardless of the environmental cues. For instance, a mouse born to fearful mice still showed extreme fear even after being reared by a fearless mouse. Human beings significantly differ in their predisposition to estimate danger and safety. This is innate, although the knowledge base and previous experiences influence it. Educational background, culture, peer interactions, social milieu, and situational circumstances modify individuals' approach toward a danger-safety dyad.

Nonetheless, it is primarily a function of psychological predisposition that can arise from underlying genetic and developmental factors. Genetic factors are presumed to be operating, and this presumption is based on the proven influence of genetic factors in some, if not all, anxiety disorders.[59] Early studies of smiling and fear in infants upon seeing strangers have shown increased concordance among monozygotic twins (genetically related twins) compared with dizygotic twins (genetically unrelated twins).[60] Similarly, the neuroticism scores were higher in monozygotic twins than in dizygotic twins.[61] Studies of twins have revealed a significant amount of heritability of phobia that varied up to 50 percent, suggesting an essential role of genetics in developing fear reactions.[62] Linkage analysis has suggested a link between panic disorder and specific chromosomes, the genetic structures.[63] Sometimes, genetic and developmental factors lie entangled, making it difficult or impossible to differentiate what is operative. For example, if parents had excess anxiety, then the growing child can also develop anxiety either in relation to genetic vulnerability or social learning from parents' anxiety during the early stages of life. Alternatively, both factors may be significant in combination.

PSYCHODYNAMIC THEORIES OF ANXIETY

It is much safer to be feared than loved because . . . love is preserved by the link of obligation which, owing to the baseness of men, is broken at every opportunity for their advantage; but fear preserves you by a dread of punishment which never fails.

—NICCOLO MACHIAVELLI

Freud's theories of anxiety had a serendipitous origin. While attending a midwife's examination, Freud came across some remarks about meconium in the amniotic fluid. The examination candidate responded that the child was frightened when asked what meconium indicated. Laughter erupted, and the candidate failed, but Freud carried it and later developed his theory that anxiety was related to the birth process. For Freud, the act of birth was the source of anxiety.

Otto Rank went deeper than his predecessors and regarded the separation of the infant from the womb and the mother as a significant biological event—the paradigmatic trauma. In his book *The Trauma of Birth*, Rank postulated that anxiety is evidence of a failed attempt to elaborate on the trauma of birth. It is so critical that every anxiety reflects the anxiety of incomplete mastery of birth trauma.

Freud initially viewed anxiety as the product of a defense mechanism of the mind called *repression. Repression is* a defense reaction that prevents instinctual but morally unacceptable wishes from entering the conscious mind from the unconscious. In this model, anxiety results from repressed libidinal or similar instincts, leading to neurotic symptoms.[64] In the second model, anxiety is the primary emotion arising from the unpleasantness of sensing unavoidable trauma, for instance, birth trauma and awareness of real and potential danger. Potential danger can include possible loss or withdrawal of the mother. Unacceptable sexual and aggressive instincts in the unconscious can result in anxiety, which, in turn, triggers *repression*. Instincts morally judged as unwelcome and uncontrollable impulses can send signals of anxiety, which, in turn, lead to the activation of psychological defenses, which are meant to deal with instincts and impulses. Freud called this anxiety "signal anxiety" as it alerts the mind about possible dangers. Sometimes, the mind becomes overwhelmed with excitation, and the subsequent anxiety experienced is known as traumatic anxiety. In the psychoanalytic framework, anxiety acts as a mechanism to regulate the expression of primary instincts. Freud regarded anxiety as either inherited or primary in that it is inherited or learned with birth. Sullivan applied the same theory but argued that interpersonal factors rather than intrapsychic agencies initiate anxiety.[65]

ATTACHMENT THEORIES

Bowlby put forward the theory of attachment.[66] According to the attachment theory, development occurs in the context of attachment behavior that is activated upon distress or expression of needs.[67] The attachment system serves an evolutionary function of seeking security from caregivers during adversity and gaining protection, thus enhancing survival. The attachment system promotes survival by offering protection in need to those who remain close in supportive roles.

Whether attachment needs are met depends on reliable and responding caregivers. Children become anxious if the care providers are not available or accessible. Attachment provides a secure base and haven for a developing child. Difficult or disorganized relation with parents leads to insecure attachment in early childhood, which, in turn, is associated with the development of anxiety in adolescence.[68]

Adult attachment styles are derived from two underlying dimensions: anxiety and avoidant. Anxiety is related to the worry about being rejected by others. Attachment reflects the extent to which people feel discomfort with closeness and intimacy.[69] In the avoidant attachment, there is a restriction on the acknowledgment of distress and attempts to seek comfort. Accordingly, there is *secure attachment* (low in anxiety and avoidance), *preoccupied attachment* (high in anxiety, low in avoidance), *fearful avoidant* (high in anxiety and avoidance), and *dismissing avoidant* (low in anxiety and high in avoidance).

Fear: The Hub for Past and Future

Fear is a unique phenomenon that represents the integration of our past and future. The genesis of fear demands the activation of memories and anticipation of consequences; the former denotes the past, and the latter is connected to the future. Damage to the hippocampus, where memory is encoded, abolishes contextual learning and subsequent fear response. For instance, animals showed fear when returning to where they were subjected to frightening stimuli. Such a fear reaction required both intact hippocampus and amygdala. Anticipation requires mental imagery of objects, visual representation of contexts with multimodal details, and a narrative structure with a sequence. In fact, these elements rely on the retrieval of past information. Humans can mentally travel backward to the past, but we actually carry the past with us while traveling forward to imagine the future. We cannot imagine our future if we cannot recall our past details. Biological studies have proven that damage to the hippocampus, the brain organ where memories are stored, affects the ability to recall events and imagine new experiences.[70] Impoverished memories imply restricted imagination. For the development of fear, memory is thus an essential requirement. However, fear is the glue that binds our past and future, and at this juncture, we should not fail to understand that the future is only a human construct, an abstract idea.

Failure of Fear Development

Life without worrying thoughts, bitten fingernails, fidgeting, trembling, or sweating is a wish for many but a reality for exceptionally few. Damage to the amygdala, the brain's fear center, and sometimes other parts results in impaired fear development.[71] Strong biological reasons are required for the complete elimination of fear. One example is Urbach-Wiethe disease, a genetic abnormality that affects the amygdala. Rachman observes that fear does not develop following exposure to all dangerous situations.[72] Several theories of fear acquisition exist, but only a few explain the lack of expected fear development. Given that fear is a powerful emotion, it cannot disappear entirely with psychological conditioning.

LIMITATIONS

Theories of fear have roots in animal studies and behavior. The appropriateness of equating animal reactions with the human experience of fear is inherently fraught with limitations. In animals, the cortical parts of the brain, mainly the prefrontal region, are less well-developed than in humans. Whether the reactions that are presumed to indicate fear are associated with the human consciousness of fear is difficult to ascertain. The same restrictions apply to the derivations of fear theories based on observations in infants and young children because the myelination of neurons takes the first few years to become functional. Therefore, the communication of the content of consciousness occurs only after a certain age. This limits the fear literature, especially our knowledge of innate fear and the stages of its development. In the same vein, studies of adults relied on self-reports of fear. One must bear in mind that self-report reflects the emotion; it can be a tail end of the broader and complex feeling state, distal and downstream.

Although based on reasoning, psychological theories such as the social learning model and psychodynamic theories are inferential rather than empirical. The behavioral theories and social learning models do not offer a uniform explanation. Some people had exposure to traumatic experiences but did not develop anxiety.[73] Even after exposure to war trauma, most victims did not have post-traumatic stress disorder.[74]

Chapter Three

Unfriendly Anxiety

Karl Jaspers, the founder of the phenomenological approach to psychiatry and a seminal figure in German existentialism, described anxiety as a feeling of restlessness irreducible to other emotions. For Jaspers, existential anxiety is fundamental to human existence, and its origin cannot be grasped.* There are two types of anxiety: one in which the subject can identify the content of anxiety and the other in which it is unattached or free-floating anxiety. The content, in this instance, means the content of consciousness. For instance, people worry about health, finances, family, or performance outcomes. These ideas occupy consciousness to become its content from time to time.

On the other hand, on many occasions, subjects cannot identify a particular content of anxiety; they experience other features of anxiety, such as an unpleasant feeling of tenseness, distress, and sometimes worry about an unknown catastrophe. Unattached anxiety may be seen in depressive disorder, generalized anxiety disorder, or psychotic syndrome but is not exclusive to these conditions. Although anxiety serves the function of harm avoidance, a state of excess vigilance or hypervigilance may lead to exaggeration of threat. As a result, an otherwise innocuous object may be perceived as threatening.

---

* Karl Jaspers writes: "It is all pervasive and dominating analogous to a vital anxiety and involving existence as a whole. There is every degree from countless, powerful anxiety that leads to a clouding of consciousness and ruthless acts of violence against oneself and others, down to a slight, anxious tension where the anxiety is experienced as alien to the self and inexplicable. Anxiety is linked with physical sensations such as pressure, suffocation and tightness."

Borkovec et al. define *worry* as a chain of thoughts with a negative emotional tone that is relatively uncontrollable; it represents an attempt to engage in mental problem-solving on an issue whose outcome is uncertain but contains the possibility of one or more negative outcomes.[1] Consequently, worry relates closely to the fear process. In this sense, worry is a broad and complex mental phenomenon encompassing ideas, emotions, and thinking (cognitive) processes. Worrying thoughts are colored by emotions and characterized by an evaluative process. Worry is more about the future than the past or present. The emotion of worry is discomfort rather than distressing. People who identified themselves as worriers were anxious and had difficulty maintaining attention. In contrast to anxiety, physiological reactions were inconspicuous in worry.

Abnormal Anxiety

Before discussing the benefits and positive aspects of anxiety, which are the main objectives of this book, let us review the negative side of anxiety, which is the traditional and perhaps instinctive notion. If there are different levels of anxiety, then where is the line drawn separating functional anxiety from abnormal anxiety? A consensual approach is based on two factors: (1) the magnitude of anxiety, and (2) the impairment from anxiety. Magnitude is understood in relative terms. Is anxiety above what can be expected in a given situation? Is it disproportionate to the source of danger? Is it so intense that it is deviant from the statistical norm? The reference may be the situation, societal norm, or even the past of the same individual. If a person experiences a level of anxiety that was never experienced before in the same situation, then for that person, it is excess anxiety. Therefore, the comparison or the frame of reference need not be anxiety reported by other individuals in society; the reference can be the same person but at different time points in life.

Impairment is defined as a deviation from habitual function. Disruption of daily functions (for example, concentration) is thus significant. In a nutshell, the distinguishing feature of morbid anxiety is that it is dysfunctional.[2] The classificatory systems in psychiatry use the term "clinically significant impairment."

Anxiety is associated with distress in individuals. Distress from anxiety also represents an impairment because it is an unwelcome state of mind. Notwithstanding, dysfunction and distress are not the same. An individual distressed with anxiety may be able to perform functions but may not be at ease.

It is the subjective evaluation of distress that is determinant in deciding whether anxiety is considered a normal experience or symptom. An analogy is a physical symptom. Pain and coughing are universal human experiences. Nonetheless, every cough or instance of pain is not a symptom, although they could represent a departure from normal physiology. Swelling in the body is a deviation from normal anatomy and still may not be a symptom. When does pain or a cough become a symptom? They become symptoms when a person feels that these deviations from the normal anatomy or physiology are so significant that a need to seek help is felt. So, symptoms are contextual in that individuals feel a need to seek medical attention. In the same vein, anxiety is a symptom when individuals feel overwhelmed by it to the extent of seeking help. This is essentially a subjective call and can vary among individuals. We should make a clear distinction here—an idea of seeking help need not translate to actual help-seeking behavior in the form of seeing a doctor or a clinical psychologist. The stigma of mental health problems, cost, access to services, or other factors may prevent people from seeking help for anxiety. Anxiety can still be a symptom regardless of seeking help because the felt need rather than the actual help-seeking behavior defines a symptom. From the above approaches based on magnitude and impairment, abnormal or morbid anxiety is anxiety that is an excess of what can be expected in a given situation or for an individual and causes impairment from either significant distress or dysfunction.

The impairment may manifest in a myriad of ways. Anxiety may cause restlessness and fatigue, which adversely affects concentration and performance. Studies have demonstrated that individuals with excess and morbid anxiety suffer from distorted memories; they may remember events representing threats more than nonthreatening situations.[3] Such preferential memory is called memory bias and is seen to affect both conscious, explicit memory and unconscious, implicit memory. Explaining it further, individuals with excess anxiety remembered more threatening words than healthy subjects without an anxiety disorder. The findings suggest that morbid anxiety can adversely affect memory and attention. Sleep disturbance may ensue from excess anxiety. Social anxiety leads to avoidance of social situations. In other situations, morbid anxiety is associated with trembling, sweating, a sensation of difficulty breathing, light-headedness, dizziness, tense muscles, and palpitations, physical experiences that can detrimentally impact day-to-day functioning. In severe situations, anxiety can lead to the experience of derealization, which is a sense of loss of feeling for the realities around. Another potential consequence is depersonalization, which is a sense of loss of feeling for the self. Extreme anxiety can paralyze organisms.

Anxiety Disorders

In medical practice, a syndrome is a constellation of symptoms and signs that occur at a frequency higher than expected by chance. Various syndromes are known in psychiatry: psychosis, mania, depression, and delirium, among others. A constellation of symptoms associated with anxiety forms anxiety syndromes. There are three commonly occurring syndromes of anxiety, as described below. The terms syndrome and disorder are used interchangeably in this context.*

1. Panic attacks: A panic attack is a sudden onset of intense episodic anxiety with physical symptoms. The intensity of anxiety may reflect in the dread of impending death, loss of control, collapse, or a catastrophic outcome. The duration of attacks may last minutes to hours. The physical symptoms are a sensation of choking, rapid breathing, chest tightness, pins and needles, dizziness, sweating, palpitation, trembling, nausea or abdominal discomfort, chills, and hot flashes. Apart from these symptoms, other atypical symptoms are also seen in clinical practice. When panic attacks are unpredictable or not associated with any particular trigger, they form panic disorder.

---

* Apart from the above syndromes, morbid anxiety may be present as a manifestation of other syndromes such as psychosis, depression, dementia, or delirium. It is noteworthy that mania is a syndrome that is mostly characterized by the absence of anxiety.

2. Phobia: A phobic reaction is a morbid anxiety associated with a specific situation or object and subsequent avoidance of the same situation, object, or endurance with distress. In this way, numerous phobias have been described in the literature: claustrophobia (phobia of closed space), social phobia (related to social situations), acrophobia (phobia of heights), and emetophobia (of vomiting) are some examples.

3. Generalized anxiety disorder: Generalized anxiety disorder is, as the term implies, morbid anxiety that is pervasive across multiple areas or themes in life, present most of the time in a day or most days in a given period. It is enduring and associated with any of the above-described symptoms. Sometimes, there may not be a specific content of anxiety, in which case anxiety is felt as unattached or free-floating anxiety.

The prevalence of anxiety disorders varies widely across the globe. According to one study, an estimated 28.8 percent of the US population had a diagnosis of an anxiety disorder in the preceding year, making it the most common psychiatric disorder.[4] The prevalence rates depend on how readily affected individuals seek help from the medical profession and participate in epidemiological surveys and also diagnostic tools used to estimate the prevalence. A systematic review of 87 studies across 44 countries found a wide prevalence range from 0.9 to 29.8 percent in the preceding year. The prevalence does not diminish appreciably with age, as anxiety disorders have comparable prevalence in the older population.[5]

The Impact of Anxiety on Physical Health, Quality of Life, and Social Well-being

Long-term studies have shown that individuals with anxiety disorders have a higher risk for heart disease than those without an anxiety disorder.[6] Such a conclusion was derived from a follow-up of subjects with anxiety for ten or more years, indicating that morbid anxiety predicted future heart disease rather than anxiety that occurred as a reaction to an existing heart disease. An estimate from 20 studies suggested a 1.26 times higher risk for heart disease with an anxiety disorder than without an anxiety disorder after adjusting for demographic variables, health behaviors, and medical factors. A Finnish follow-up study showed two times increased risk of raised inflammatory makers with anxiety.[7] Evidence suggests a detrimental impact of anxiety disorders on quality of life and social functioning.[8] A systematic review and meta-analysis found that the direct cost of anxiety disorders was 2.08 percent of health care costs and 0.22 percent of gross domestic product (GDP), whereas indirect costs, on average, corresponded to 0.23 percent of GDP. In addition to the population-level health cost, the cost to the individual patients was significantly higher compared with the healthy control groups.[9] Severe anxiety can be associated with reduced job opportunities and impaired performance at work, in addition to reduced participation from laborers.[10] Anxiety disorders are the sixth leading cause of person-years lived with disability, a measure of disability.

Anxiety disorders are common in childhood and adolescence and are also linked to considerable adverse impacts on future life. The famous Great Smoky Mountains Study estimated that 22.7 percent of young people suffered from one or more anxiety disorders by age 26.[11] Morbid anxiety in adolescents was found to be associated with future risks of anxiety disorder, major depression, educational underachievement, and early parenthood in the youth.[12] The Great Smoky Mountains Study demonstrated that anxiety disorders in childhood were associated with adverse functioning in one or more of the following domains in adulthood: interpersonal, health, and/or financial.

Mental disorders are associated with stigma in society, and anxiety disorders are no exception. People view anxiety as a character weakness.[13] There is also a notion that those who are anxious can get out of their anxiety as if anxiety is under their control. This view may be reinforced and perpetuated by the apparent senselessness of morbid anxiety. For these reasons, people may hide their anxiety, leading to underdiagnosis.

SOCIAL FEAR

Although fear is a universal reaction, its expression is modified by cultures and practices that vary across periods. In the modern world, societies face collective anxiety. Its content varies from natural calamities to conflicts and wars through road accidents, cot death, crimes, and pandemics. When science brings technology and makes human life safer and more comfortable than before, one should not intuitively think that fear will also subside. It does not. The age of enlightenment and reason replaced superstitions and evil spirits, but in their place came massive weapons and the prices of technology, such as climate change. Guns can be as frightening as the witchcraft that science and technology replaced. The gap between the beliefs of the lay public and science forms a fertile ground for further social anxiety. With social anxiety, everyday life is restructured. Anxiety, being highly contagious, spreads through media and personal contacts. Collective anxiety leads to collective efforts intended to mitigate dangers.

The COVID-19 pandemic embodies collective anxiety. First, the pandemic was perceived as everyone's problem. There was also an understanding that no one or no country was safe until everyone was safe. Anxiety became social, a phenomenon with a recognition that everyone was confronting the same danger. The pandemic paved the way for large-scale cautionary measures at an unprecedented scale—isolation, travel restrictions, closures of public spaces, wearing of face masks, and accelerated development of vaccines. Anxiety was felt in every corner as everyone's predicament. Although the content is different, climate changes and natural calamities can produce the same level of reactions at a global level. In a way, this is global anxiety. The anxiety of terrorism resulting in security screening is another example of collective anxiety. The promotion of electric vehicles, organic food, and lifestyle gymnasiums represents adaptive responses to social anxiety related to climate changes and health risks.

In summary, excess anxiety can be impairing and morbid. Anxiety disorders cause a huge burden on human life, seriously compromising the quality of life. Morbid anxiety is distressing and disabling. With extreme or enduring morbid anxiety, vigor can be sapped. It then becomes the most meaningless misery for humans.

Avoidant Behavior, Cost, and Loss of Rewards

The behavior of avoidance of potential and perceived threats is central to morbid anxiety.[14] Avoidance is seen toward cues that signal threats, which signaled threats in the past, not currently, and contexts associated with threats.[15] With anxiety, there is a predilection for threatening stimuli that will be selectively processed during thinking. The associated emotional reactions are also prominent in avoidance behavior. Empirical data from human experiments show that with a high level of anxiety, people miss advantages and rewards because of avoidant behavior. With repeated or increasing avoidance, anxiety will not be eliminated; it may even be strengthened. As a result, individuals may not be able to pursue their goals and suffer from a lack of opportunities when situations are nonthreatening and advantageous. Incidental anxiety is anxiety that is related to environmental factors that are unrelated to current affairs.[16] Incidental anxiety can affect decision-making, and this phenomenon is known as the affect heuristic. For instance, a person who experiences a car accident carries the anxiety related to the accident, which later affects decisions that are unrelated to the accident. There is a misattribution to the source of anxiety. Individuals with a high level of anxiety engage in an adult attachment style characterized by overinvolvement, overprotection, and intrusive and controlling behavior.[17] This style may thwart the development of autonomy and promote dependency. Also, morbid anxiety affects not only the individual but also intimate relationships. An association between anxiety disorders and a partner's marital stress has been documented.[18]

Chapter Four

Neurobiology of Fear

There are two distinct aspects of fear. First, there are fear responses. Secondly, there are brain operations that generate fear responses and occur outside the realm of consciousness. These two systems, proposed by LeDoux and Pine, offer a heuristic convenience for our understanding of fear and have implications for treating anxiety disorders.[1] The unconscious fear process commences when the sensory neurons detect a threat. This innate response is familiar to mammalian brains and has been preserved across various species in the animal kingdom. This system of unconscious fear operates based on many chemicals and structures in the brain. For explanation, one chemical—corticotrophin-releasing hormone—and one brain structure—the amygdala—require further elaboration in the remaining parts of this chapter.

The outcome of the fear process is fear response. Fear responses include fear reactions and a conscious experience of fear. Fear reactions manifest in physiological symptoms and avoidant behavior. The physiological symptoms in this instance are the same phenomenon we dealt with in the first chapter: palpitation, sweating, trembling, rapid breathing, and similar signs. There are two types of fear reactions: conscious and unconscious ones. The unconscious fear reactions can occur without the conscious feeling of fear, which originates from the most evolved and advanced part of the brain: the neocortex. The amygdala lies beneath the larger neocortex.

FEAR AND ANXIETY REACTIONS

The corticotrophin-releasing hormone (CRH) is the most studied brain chemical involved in the fear response. Activation of this hormone ultimately results in enhanced production of steroids in the body, which prepares the organisms to face danger. Steroids are produced by the adrenal glands placed above the kidneys, but the messenger for production—CRH—comes from the brain. CRH also acts in brain centers that control the release of noradrenaline, another stress chemical. Noradrenaline, like steroids, helps organisms deal with threatening stimuli or objects. In this manner, CRH controls physiological and behavioral responses to fear.

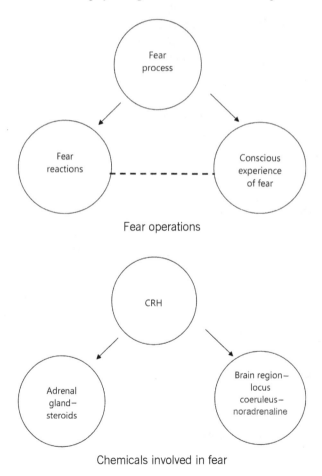

Fear operations

Chemicals involved in fear

Noradrenaline is produced in a brain structure called the locus coeruleus. Despite its extensive connections and widespread influences on the cortical brain, the locus coeruleus is a small structure composed of 25,000 to 90,000 neurons. When the noradrenaline level in the brain falls, that leads to drowsiness and reduced alertness. In the normal awake state, noradrenaline suppresses neuronal firing related to spontaneous activities, associations within the brain, and contexts other than stimuli that are presented to consciousness, called salient stimuli. In other words, irrelevant background information is attenuated and alertness is maintained.[2] In a nutshell, noradrenaline has widespread suppressing action on cortical neurons, except the neurons that process stimuli presented to the circuits of the brain which process conscious awareness. The final effect is filtering out irrelevant stimuli and indirectly streaming salient stimuli. The activity of locus coeruleus and its interaction with the amygdala plays an essential role in threat learning. Excess activity of noradrenaline leads to over-suppression of background activity, which may create a sense of inability to use past information to orientate consciousness to the new event. An appraisal of the inability to control response to the new event is potentially threatening. Such a state is associated with morbid anxiety and panic reaction. The normal cortical control of the subcortical influence of noradrenaline will be lost during a panic attack.

The differential views of *fear* and *anxiety*, as briefly encountered in chapter 1, have a conceptual base and neurobiological substrates. Fear is phasic, an immediate reaction to a real threat. Anxiety is an enduring response to an uncertain but potentially dangerous situation. While the amygdala mediates fear response, the brain structure involved in anxiety is called the bed nucleus of stria terminalis (BNST). The BNST is activated when the threat is loosely defined, not proximal, but lingering over time. For example, a storm induces fear and is a real threat. However, even after the storm is over, people may be anxious about the next storm. Such an unpleasant, aversive mental state may last longer, although it is not based on an actual or imminent threat. Such anticipatory anxiety is related to the activation of BNST. An intriguing finding from a brain scan study was that the activation of BNST produced anticipatory anxiety without activating the amygdala.[3]

On the other hand, when a threatening stimulus was placed close to the subjects, the amygdala and BNST were activated, implying that the actual and proximal threats produced broad and diffuse activation of fear regions and circuits. In contrast, distant and imagined threat activates BNST rather than the amygdala.[4] Additionally, unpredictable shock in experimental settings and a sense of loss of control activated BNST, suggesting its role in sustained anxiety.[5] In individuals with a high level of anxiety, the activity of BNST was associated with hypervigilance.[6]

Grillion et al. have further elaborated the concepts of reactions to explicit cues of threats in contrast to the reactions to the environment or contexts in which such cues were placed. For example, when a bell is associated with electric shock, the former becomes a conditioned stimulus that elicits a conditioned response of fear. In addition, animals learn about the environment (e.g., a cage, a room, or other situations) in which the conditioned stimulus occurs. Reactions to such environments or contexts which imply potential threats, not the actual ones, can be sustained. This is known as *context conditioning*. The fear conditioning in response to definite threats and context conditioning in response to exposure to the context in which threats appeared depend on the activation of the amygdala. However, context conditioning also requires the hippocampus and BNST. In other words, the phasic cue-related reaction is fear that is brought by the amygdala, and the sustained contextual reaction is anxiety, which the amygdala, hippocampus, and BNST mediate.

The role of BNST is further supported by known mechanisms of medications used to treat anxiety. Serotonin is one of the most well-known neurochemicals related to anxiety. Apropos of the above findings, the BNST is rich with serotonin receptors where antianxiety medications exert their actions. These medications are called selective serotonin reuptake inhibitors (SSRIs). In the same vein, another neurochemical, GABA, is the target of the powerful anxiolytic medications known as benzodiazepines. GABA is abundant in BNST. It is noteworthy that chronic administration of SSRIs and benzodiazepines abolishes anxiety but not fear of the real threat. Studies of benzodiazepines showed their beneficial effects on sustained, anticipatory fear (akin to anxiety) but not cue-related fear.[7] For these reasons, antianxiety medications are less effective against phobia where excess fear, although irrational, is related to specific cues, objects, or situations.[8] Systematic and repeated exposure is the preferred therapy in this instance, as it may lead to the extinction of fear through desensitization to fear-provoking situations. Mounting evidence has thus shifted the landscape of neurology of anxiety from amygdala—the center of fear response—to BNST and points toward different brain systems for fear and anxiety.

There is no single isolated fear center in the brain nor any solitary fear circuit. Thus, activation of the amygdala stimulates neurons that express corticotropin-releasing hormone (CRH).[9] There is an abundance of CRH neurons in the central nucleus of the amygdala. These neurons project to the brain region that regulates noradrenaline and the hypothalamus. The CRH activates the hypothalamic-pituitary-adrenal axis, the human cardinal stress response system. Although CRH is produced in the hypothalamus, the amygdala is the origin of the CRH pathway, and the activation of the central nucleus of the amygdala is essential for the stress response. Direct injection of CRH into the amygdala has been proven to produce fear and stress reactions in experiments.

Conversely, chemical blockers of CRH reduce anxiety. The projections of CRH neurons from the amygdala to *locus coeruleus*, the noradrenaline-regulating brain region, stimulate noradrenaline production. Noradrenaline brings physical anxiety symptoms, such as palpitation, rapid breathing, chest tightness, and sweating.[10] The fear response is thus a product of multiple interacting brain systems. Nonetheless, the amygdala is viewed as a hub upon and from which several common neuronal pathways converge and originate.

Despite the above differences between fear and anxiety, these phenomena lie along a continuum. Humans have the power of imagination. When people anticipate a threat, it is akin to facing it. Such an anticipated threat (anxiety) stimulates the same reactions as fear but is less intense than the actual threat.[11] As mentioned above, antianxiety medications are less effective against phobia characterized by excess fear, which is related to a specific object or situation.[12]

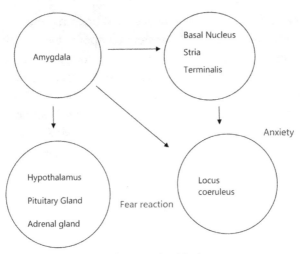

Structures involved in fear

DISSOCIATION BETWEEN SUBJECTIVE FEELING OF FEAR AND OBJECTIVE REACTIONS OF FEAR

The biology of fear we have so far discussed is all about fear or anxiety reactions. They are primarily objective in that fear and anxiety reactions—physiological and avoidance behavior—can be perceived by human observation. Physiological reactions such as increased heart rate, sweating, trembling, and rapid breathing are observable phenomena, as well as avoidant behavior such as receding and withdrawal. These reactions are to be differentiated from the feeling of fear, which is the essential emotional aspect, and for all purposes, fear proper. Fear is fundamentally a subjective conscious awareness, an unpleasant feeling.

The caveat is that living organisms may exhibit fear reactions without experiencing the feeling of fear. The converse is also true; people feel fear without showing overt fear reactions. Damage to the amygdala eliminates fear reactions, but it is known that feeling of fear persists in such instances. Similarly, the BNST activity produces anxiety responses—detection of unpredictable and potential threats and prepares the organisms for defensive behavior. The BNST in itself does not generate conscious feelings of anxiety. So, what brings conscious experiential fear, the actual feeling of fear?

Luu and colleagues describe widespread brain representation of anxiety.[13] We have already seen a brainstem component—an activating noradrenergic system, hypothalamic defensive system, and limbic emotional and memory control system. According to Luu et al., higher cortical regions, such as the frontal lobes, are involved in the conscious experience of anxiety. An example is apathy, which is a state of complete absence of emotions. Apathy results from frontal lobe damage. Affected victims do not show any concern or emotion. For them, fear is either meaningless or nonexistent. Damage in other parts of the frontal lobe causes a lack of inhibition (disinhibited behavior), again indicating a lack of fear of consequences. Luu et al. argue that the role of the frontal lobe in the operation of anxiety is significant in that it is the frontal lobe function, specifically working memory, that mediates the response to fear. Anxiety informs, alerts higher cortical structures, and directs evaluative processes toward a threatening stimulus.

Neurosurgeons who performed brain surgery for intractable epilepsy noted that removing a part of the frontal lobe affected the behavior of their patients. After surgery, some of them became risk-taking and impulsive. Additionally, there was an attitude of acting according to "the here and now" rather than showing forward-looking decision-making. Imagination was still intact, but there was a deficiency in pleasure and discomfort. These findings led to the hypothesis that emotions, including discomfort and possibly anxiety, are imperative in planning. Consciously experienced fear is associated with activation in several brain regions, viz., parietal, frontal, and temporal lobes, which is different from the activation associated with unconscious fear reactions.[14]

CHAPTER FIVE

Psychological Theories and Philosophy of Fear

LIKE OTHER FEATURES OF LIVING CREATURES, EMOTIONS ARE VIEWED AS products of evolution. Emotions helped the survival of various species and thus were preserved over time. Emotions are broadly divided into two: appetitive and aversive. They have two dimensions: quality and quantity. Quality refers to valence of emotion, either negative or positive. It is negative, as in aversive emotions, such as fear, or positive, as in appetitive emotions, such as happiness. Arousal is a reflection of the intensity of emotion. Emotions in less-evolved organisms are relatively simple compared with humans; they lead to approaching behavior to appetitive stimuli and withdrawal from aversive stimuli. With more evolved organisms such as humans, the physiological aspect of emotions—the autonomous signs such as palpitation and tremor—are also manifest. Unique expressions in language and physiological and behavioral expressions characterize emotions in the most evolved humans. Moreover, response inhibition of emotional expression is peculiar to humans. Humans can not only express love in roses and poems but also suppress the manifestations of anger.

Emotions represent certain predispositions in humans, not necessarily expressions. They prepare humans for actions that may or may not be discharged. For example, a person may feel love and aroused but remain quiet without action or fear but without flight. They are thus preparatory, not always reactionary.

JUDGMENTAL BIAS

The fundamental bias in anxiety is overestimating the probability of harm and underestimating safety.[1] Additionally, the estimate of the cost of an untoward outcome (for example, injury) is also associated with anxiety.[2] The overestimation of the cost of danger is more relevant for anxiety than the estimate of the probability of danger itself.[3] These inflated estimates represent judgmental biases in anxiety and serve as mechanistic models for further studies. For Barlow, the most critical component is a sense of uncontrollability over future anticipated threats.[4] Stretching it further, anxiety involves a sense of helplessness because the future connotes unpredictability and uncertainty.[5] These biases in anxiety may impair information processing and decision-making. With a high level of anxiety, impairment in decision-making for tasks that involve risk increases with a high level of ambiguity. Although anxiety impairs the validity of judgments, there is a propensity for less risky choices with increasing ambiguity. Smith et al. observe that it is the level of ambiguity that mediates less risky decisions during anxiety. Smith et al. observe that it is the level of ambiguity that mediates less risky decisions during anxiety.[6] At the same time, evidence suggests that anxiety is a cause rather than a consequence of negative predictions.[7] People become anxious first and then make pessimistic predictions rather than making negative predictions and becoming anxious.

DEVIATION FROM HABITUAL PATTERN AND DISCREPANCY

Hebb proposed that fear resulted from the discrepancy in expectations from habitual patterns and perception. This can lead to confusion and loss of control. An example of such a situation is a disruption in the planned travel route. According to Hebb, this is accompanied by a profound disorganization of cerebral processes.

ATTENTIONAL BIAS AND EVALUATIVE MEANING

Individuals with a high level of anxiety have a predilection for attention biased toward threat-related cues and events, even when they are irrelevant. Given that the resources for attention are limited, there is an attentional bias in anxiety so that attention may be diverted to irrelevant threats with consequent attention deficits for relevant stimuli. There is also a propensity to interpret ambiguous stimuli as more threatening and expect adverse outcomes.

Features of inborn fear were discussed in chapter 2. Accordingly, fear reactions develop without analysis of the meaning of the stimulus; certain stimuli evoke fear instantaneously.* In addition to inborn fear, conditioned fear also develops suddenly, and the learning is implicit, not the result of conscious attribution of meaning. Infants and animals at the lower level of the evolutionary ladder show fear reactions. However, there is no evidence to conclude that there is an evaluative process of the frightening stimulus.

On the other hand, grown-up humans can attain and attribute meaning to objects and situations, whether threatening or reassuring. The meaning of the situation, its appraisal, and the thought are generally known as cognitive processing. For example, attributing the meaning of a remedy to a medication can be reassuring, whereas the meaning of a poison, a serious side effect, can generate anxiety. Whether emotions, especially anxiety, develop without attribution of meaning to the stimulus, the cognitive process is unknown.

UNCERTAINTY AND ANXIETY

The essence of anxiety lies in the sense of uncertainty.[8] Therefore, our tasks will not be complete without discussing uncertainty. There is no scope here to discuss the varying definitions of uncertainty. Defined simply, uncertainty is a lack of knowledge about some aspect of reality.[9] In this sense, it is purely a state of mind, not a feature of the objective world. However, uncertainty is not a lack of knowledge alone; it is an awareness, a conscious experience of not knowing. The experiential aspect is consequential because it arouses emotions and leads to behaviors—the actions. Uncertainty manifests as indeterminateness, unpredictability, indefiniteness, and likewise. Uncertainty in the form of an epistemic gap characterizes the evaluative content of anxiety.[10]

---

* Barlow remarks: "Anxiety is a sense of uncontrollability focused largely on possible future threats, danger, or other upcoming potentially negative events, in contrast to fear, where the danger is present and imminent."

Uncertainty results when people cannot make subjective interpretations of realities or make a structure of events.[11] This is an inability to form a mental sketch of events. Uncertainty has multiple origins. It can originate from ambiguity caused by changing patterns, observations that turn out to be inaccurate, and events that are vague and lacking salience. Novelty or lack of familiarity can generate uncertainty, as does the complexity of situations or objects. A lack of congruence of events and dissonance between what was anticipated and what occurred can lead to uncertainty.

Lack of congruence indicates instability and unpredictability. A person's mental capacity to pay attention to stimuli and process information is not limitless. When mental resources are deficient or exhausted, uncertainty occurs.

In spite of the central role of uncertainty in anxiety, anxious situations can become complex. As Vazard asks, is uncertainty intrinsic to anxiety?[12] People often possess knowledge of the situations they are exposed to but can still be anxious. For instance, one may be anxious about giving a public speech. Vazard argues that uncertainty sometimes lies in the fine-grained features of situations, such as what exactly will happen and how and when an untoward incident is going to occur. Also, uncertainties involve one's ability to cope with adverse outcomes and events. Uncertainty has, therefore, a complex and varied dimension.

Uncertainty is understandably unpleasant, given that it reduces the human ability to manipulate past and present information to increase the odds of desired future outcomes. Such an inability implies a degree of uncontrollability as well. Given that anxiety arises from a lack of certainty and control over threatening situations, one way to deal with it is to reduce the threat or terminate it and gain controllability.[13] This is called pragmatic control.[14] Even an illusion of control is known to reduce anxiety. In an experimental situation, when subjects were instructed that they had control over the amount of carbon dioxide they received, anxiety symptoms were found to be fewer compared with symptoms in those who believed they had no control.[15] Another mechanism is to enhance knowledge and increase the power to predict the future. Increased predictability brings epistemic control.

The easiest approach to handling uncertainty is imagination. Response to uncertainty is thus anticipation of an imagined future outcome; it could be negative, positive, or even neutral. If a person anticipates a negative outcome, then preparatory defense mechanisms will be activated, which will be more effective in case a threat occurs but unnecessary if the threat does not occur. So, the benefit is its effectiveness in the case of an actual threat, but its downside is its cost if there is no actual threat.

On the other hand, with anticipation of a positive outcome and no preparatory actions, defensive reactions will be less effective in the event of a threat. If there is no actual threat, such responses will be more efficient as unnecessary mobilization of resources can be avoided. Anxiety is the product of an inclination toward more effective preparatory actions with anticipation of a negative outcome.

There is preferential attention to threatening stimuli over neutral or reassuring stimuli in anxious individuals.[16] Grupe and Nitschke proposed several mechanisms for the generation of anxiety: inflated estimates of threat probability and subsequent increased attention to threat and hypervigilance, deficient safety learning, and heightened reactivity to threat uncertainty.[17]

ANXIETY REACTIONS

Marks and Nesse proposed four different types of anxiety reactions and placed them akin to the immune system.[18] They include the following: (1) Escape (flight) or avoidance: Through escape or avoidance, the dangerous stimulus is kept at a distance. This is similar to vomiting or diarrhea, which keeps pathogens away; (2) Aggressive defense (anger, clawing, biting, or spraying with noxious substances): This reaction harms the source of the danger or eliminates it just as the immune system attacks bacteria; (3) Freezing/immobility may benefit by (a) aiding location and assessment of the danger, (b) concealment, and (c) inhibiting the predator's attack reflex; and finally, (4) submission/appeasement is useful when the threat comes from one's group or an opponent stronger than oneself. These responses survived probably because they increased fitness. Nausea and vomiting, although unpleasant, survived as a way to eliminate food that could be toxic. In the same way, reactions associated with anxiety increase survival by distancing, avoiding, or eliminating the danger.

A unique aspect of anxiety reaction is that it responds to cues and signs of danger rather than the complete exposure to danger. Signs of fire or the sight of a snake can also cause anxiety. To become anxious, one does not need to wait for burns from fire or a bite from a snake. A storm forecast is sufficient to induce anxiety before the real storm hits. The anxiety reaction is thus semiotic. The mind reads the hints and then reacts. Marks and Nesse argue that our predecessors have survived by reading these hints, and the present generations do not need to suffer from the necessity to learn from bitter experiences. Organisms that responded to dangerous cues rather than the occurrence of dangers likely had better survival and comparatively more decedents than those who did not respond. The brain is wired so that responses that predated the occurrence of dangers were selected during evolution. The hints of threat thus attract attention, which is known as prepotency or salience.

Another observation that supports the adaptive value of anxiety is its temporal occurrence. Fear of heights and falls develops when infants start to crawl, which increases with further crawling experience. Fear of animals emerges when a child starts exploring the outside world. Similarly, no anxiety occurs in response to nonthreatening objects such as leaves, flowers, or clouds. Also, in support of the evolutionarily shaped anxiety, modern dangers such as road traffic, inappropriate use of recreational drugs, or pandemics do not induce as much fear as crude ancient stimuli such as heights, snakes, or loud noise. This is because evolution is time-consuming, and the genetic endowment is currently insufficient to produce robust anxiety responses to newly emerged threats. At the same time, these dangers are not entirely devoid of anxiety; they are associated with a certain degree of anxiety, although not as instantaneous or strong as ancient stimuli, suggesting that a gradual process is taking place; individuals learn and acquire fear as they are exposed to these dangers. The timescale for evolutionary adaptation is considerably long and difficult to estimate precisely.

Are emotions inborn and inherited? There are contrasting views on this. The idea that emotions are different and discrete so that one is distinguished from another is centuries old. Darwin pointed out different facial, physiological, and behavioral features of distinct emotions, their functions, and their evolution. Following Darwin's theory, Silvan Tomkins proposed that basic emotions are seen in all cultures (pancultural).[19] These basic emotions are surprise, interest, joy, rage, fear, disgust, shame, and anguish. Ekman and Izard tested Tomkin's hypothesis with cross-cultural studies and found that people across cultures expressed and recognized emotions similarly.[20] The concept of separate emotions with distinguishing features formed discrete emotion theory. Tomkins argued that emotions are products of evolution and genetically determined.[21] The affect program is a concept that originated from the work of Tomkins. Affect program is a brain representation of responses produced by emotions. The proponents of discrete emotion theory argue that clustering of responses, viz., facial, muscular, autonomic, and vocal, differentiates different emotions as distinct entities, and they are given in nature, not acquired.

The opponents of the natural inheritance of emotions challenge the discrete emotion theory. They argue that there is no strong correlation between one particular emotion and the corresponding brain system; different brain areas process the same emotion, indicating a lack of specificity or uniqueness. The correlation of expression of the same emotion among individuals is not as high as one would expect. Therefore, in place of a natural kind of emotions, there is an alternate view—emotions are psychological constructs developed through cultures and languages. In *Anxious: Using the Brain to Understand and Treat Fear and Anxiety*[22], Joseph LeDoux argues that conscious and cognitive processes, rather than prepackaged inborn systems, are imperative for emotions.

It is challenging to solve whether emotions are inborn or learned and acquired from experiences, cultures, language, and cognitive processes. Taking a critical view of the above debate, both sides focus on two different aspects of the same process. The inherited view of emotions has every reason to suppose that they are products of the nervous system. It is a fundamental principle that the function of an organ is a function of its structure. If the nervous system and its anatomy are uniform across individuals, then its functions must also be the same, and emotions are no exception. Moreover, in the real world, it is a common observation that people experience and express emotions in more or less the same manner. So, we have the hardware—the brain—as the foundation of emotions.

The wire fires with environmental triggers. Environment and the timing of triggers are variable. Variations in the expression of emotions thus occur across individuals. Cultural practices and linguistic differences influence the expression of emotions. Cognitive evaluation and memories, unique to an individual, are essential components of emotion generation. In this way, the opposition against the natural kind of emotions holds.

Nonetheless, these variations act on a relatively uniform neural structure—the brain—without which emotions cannot arise. In other words, emotions are neither purely innate nor exclusively acquired. They are products of both processes. An important factor not considered in the earlier debate was growing evidence of a genetic relationship with emotions. Whether emotion variations can be attributed to gene sequences is a pertinent question. Although with limited findings, there is an indication that genetic variations were associated with emotionally enhanced vividness.[23] The heritability of emotions is discussed elsewhere.[24] These findings point toward the inherited basis of emotions.

Fear, The Feeling

The fundamental feature of fear or anxiety is the unpleasant feeling of it. It is also characterized by a sense of threat and an awareness of danger. While fear reactions can be innate, a feeling of fear, LeDoux argues, is a learned phenomenon, not an inborn one. Children learn what it is like to feel fear from their experiences, parents' social models, and language. Children, for instance, associate words such as "nervousness," "fear," "anxiety," and "worry" with bodily manifestations and threat situations. Experiences attached to emotions are stored in memory as emotional concepts.

While defining or describing the conscious feeling of fear is difficult, LeDoux explains the ingredients of emotions with a specific emphasis on fear. The first ingredient is awareness of the threat. Awareness is consciousness. The second ingredient is the physiological reactions brought by the activation of the defensive survival circuit (as we have seen in chapter 1, physiological reactions are components of emotions). The third ingredient is attention to the threat, and the fourth is memory. *Memory* is the information stored in the brain. Fear of fire arises from the memory of fire, the information that fire can destroy property and lives. This is stored information; in other words, it is a memory. This type of memory is related to knowledge and is known as semantic memory. This ingredient is essential to generate a conscious feeling of fear. Lastly, a cognitive, evaluative process, the meaning of the threat, and its implications complete the ingredients. The brain cortex processes these ingredients to eventually generate the conscious feeling of fear. Language or symbols are critical in this process. These ingredients, such as awareness, attention, or memory, are not necessarily exclusive to the emotion of fear. LeDoux argues that the ingredients of emotions are nonemotional.

The above-described feeling of emotion is different from reactions to emotions. Fear reactions are thus different from fear feelings. The former results from the brain region lying below the topmost cortical brain. This subcortical brain region, as a rule, develops before the topmost cortical region. Phylogenetically, the same sequence followed. Lower brain comes first before the higher brain. In infants, the subcortical brain exists without a fully matured cortical brain. Therefore, infants show fear reactions without fear feeling. The feeling of fear is learned later in life. It is a product of processing in the most-evolved topmost cortex.

The Conscious Experience of Fear

LeDoux argues that neither the amygdala nor BNST is solely responsible for the subjective feeling of fear. Conscious experience arises when higher-order cortical brain regions give meaning to the lower-order nonconscious processes. There are cortical brain regions and circuits that represent corresponding subcortical regions and circuits. The cortical brain regions are collectively known as the association cortex, and specifically, they are the inner and outer parts of the front part of the brain (called the frontal cortex). Also, according to brain scans, frontal and parietal areas were activated when humans were conscious of a visual threat; when the threat degraded, the activities diminished.

It is proposed that the difference between nonemotional and emotional conscious awareness results from the input signals the cortical brain receives. When the cortex processes input from the amygdala and related subcortical regions, the consciousness of fear ensues. On a broader dimension, fear and anxiety are generated not only in relation to predators or immediate dangers but also to distant threats such as fear of starvation, future death, or reputational damage. Such a broad framework of fear and anxiety suggests a cognitive process, evaluative meaning, and interpretation of stimuli passed on to the brain cortex. Insula is part of the cortex that interprets the signals arising from the body, generating consciousness of body sensations. With available knowledge, it seems that language is unique to humans. Language is the vehicle of thought. Consciousness is always consciousness of something: its content. The content of consciousness expresses itself in language and symbols. Conscious feelings of fear and anxiety are thus processed and expressed with the help of language.

In real life, the experience of fear is not compartmentalized according to the above theoretical frameworks. Fear is a unified experience. It entails awareness of the unpleasant feeling, accompanied by fear reactions, especially physiological ones such as sweating, palpitation and trembling, and worrying thoughts of untoward outcomes in the future. The intensity of these components may vary, and as mentioned before in the introductory chapter, sometimes, there may not be any specific content of worrying thought. More discussions about the experiential aspects of anxiety take us to the next topic: philosophical descriptions.

Philosophical Aspects of Fear and Anxiety

We have seen that anxiety invariably embraces uncertainty. It is a fundamental human desire to resolve the feeling of uncertainty. Philosophy makes inquiries into uncertainty and mysteries and seeks meaning. Anxiety becomes an essential predisposition toward curiosity. It is, therefore, understandable that anxiety is linked to various philosophies.

Søren Kierkegaard, the founder of existentialism, presents "dread" [*angste*] as different from fear in that the dread is unfocused and overwhelming.[25] It has some similarities with anxiety but is more than anxiety. If a man has never been in dread, then for Kierkegaard, that man is spiritless. He writes: "Greater the dread, the greater the man." Dread is the dread of possibilities and freedom. Kierkegaard exemplifies a man standing on the edge of a cliff. (Let us keep the inherent fear of heights aside. We are considering the conscious and hermeneutic aspects of this situation.) The terror arises from the possibility of falling. The man can stay but is also aware of the possibility of intentionally throwing himself from the cliff. He has the freedom to choose, but this freedom to choose from possibilities itself is terrifying. Kierkegaard conceptualizes dread as the "dizziness of freedom." The dread that conflicts between possibilities and freedom is existential. This is intensified by a lack of objective evidence to know the best choice and the inability to forestall the consequences of choice. A person faces damnation if he acts. He is also damned if he does not act, as one has personal responsibility for action. Anxiety informs us of choices, however. When Adam was instructed not to eat the forbidden fruit, it implied the possibility of eating it. Adam can obey God or eat the fruit. This conflict generates dread. For Kierkegaard, anxiety precedes sin.

The possibilities are educative. Humans go through various stages of ignorance and purposelessly test multiple possibilities. We can also be responsible and thoughtful. Anxiety can lead to paralysis and inaction but can also trigger creativity and eventual salvation by attaining faith in eternal values. When a man finds repose in the faith, dread disappears. "For him, dread becomes a serviceable spirit." Dread alarms man about the next instance; through dread, possibilities become educative for fitness and finite relationships. Whoever has learned to be anxious the right way has learned the ultimate. Mawson suggests that through anxiety, humans bear the painful existence and realities and thus acquire opportunities to grow.[26] At the heart of existential fear is thanatophobia—the fear of nonbeing and nothingness.

For Sartre, upon experiencing fear, one remains conscious of the world rather than one's own self. Fear is connected to the outside world and is thus nonreflective of the self. When fear reactions cause fainting or freezing, a magical transformation of the outside world occurs. Nietzsche contended that the fear of one's neighbor creates the perspective for moral valuation.[27] When a community is secured against external dangers, the internal dangers are contained by fear, bringing morality. Fear taught man to submit himself for the mercy of nature. Nietzsche asks, has the world not lost its charm when we became less fearful? Before Nietzsche, Thomas Hobbes held that civilized societies took their origin not in the mutual goodwill of men but in fear that men had against each other.[28] Without a common power or authority to keep people in awe, everyone would have been at war with one another, but fear, as Hobbes shows, preserved societies. Fear thus became a source of peace, not war. Hobbes admitted that compassion for others existed, but it was weaker than instincts of self-preservation and conflicts. Although Hobbes stated that men lived in constant fear of each other, the primary fear was the fear of the unknown: the natural world.

Svendsen contends that a world without fear would be deadly boring.[29] Fear fills entertainment programs and activities. We experience fear while watching horror films, reading fiction, and riding a terrifying roller coaster. Why? There are alternate pleasant emotions for us to cherish. Still, we are after frightening experiences. A difference between these voluntarily induced fear and other fear situations is that we have a sense of control over voluntary fear. We experience fear from a distance, Svendsen points out. Voluntarily induced fear represents an attempt to master real-life fear. In such instances, a small amount of controlled fear, especially with repeated experiences, may act like a vaccine over time, and people may develop mastery of fear.

Existential Anxiety

For Kierkegaard, anxiety was at the root of human existence; for others, it is essential to be human.*[30] However, considering the ubiquitous nature of anxiety across species, anxiety is fundamental to living. According to Heidegger, anxiety is related to the confrontation with the meaningless universe. Human perceptions are interpretations, not absolute reality. All meanings are relative. Human beings are the creators of these meanings. Anxiety is revealed in identifying the finitude of existence and inevitability of death with which all meanings will end. Acceptance of the truth of

---

* In *Being and Nothingness*, Sartre observes: "My anxiety is distinguished from fear in that fear is fear of being in the world, whereas anxiety is anxiety before myself."

nothingness and anxiety makes people real individuals. Denial or escape from anxiety results in an inauthentic life. Echoing these thoughts, Tyrer has written that anxiety is not abhorred, for a world without anxiety will be bored and filled with frustration and torpor.[31]

Anxiety and Fear in Art and Literature

Fear has colored human encounters from the primeval to postmodern art and literature and served as an essential ingredient of creations. Dostoyevsky's Raskolnikov (in *Crime and Punishment*) and Sartre's Pablo Ibbietta (in "The Wall") reflect the fear of impending doom, the unknowable, and uncertainty. Terror and death were the defining themes of Gothic fiction. Tillich argued that anxiety is a reaction to the ever-present threat of everlasting termination of man's being. Other philosophers described anxiety in relation to the dissolution of the self.[32]

Does fear represent love? Thomas Aquinas argues that fear comes from the love of something.[33] Fear is the fear of losing something loved or wanted. A mental state characterized by a complete lack of emotions is called *apathy*. A person with apathy does not experience any interest in color, beauty, romance, or life itself. The most striking feature of apathy is not the emotional void itself but a lack of concern for it. We can and should presume that apathy also implies a lack of fear. A man with no interest or love has nothing to lose and cannot be fearful. Being in love bears the potential loss of love and the fear of abandonment. Love is subsumed in fear.

Is fear connected to hope? Once perdition becomes sure to be imminent, its future connotation is lost, and Aquinas observes that when all hope is gone, there is no need for fear. Anxiety, it is argued, is generated by the uncertainty of the future, the unknown that implies danger as one possibility. Should we, therefore, infer that anxiety will cease upon facing inevitable and imminent destruction, an utterly hopeless situation? Or is there hope if there is anxiety? Svendsen denies any strictly necessary link between fear and hope; as described earlier, fear is a reaction to actual, imminent, and inevitable threats.[34] It will remain, perhaps with more intensity, as the threat becomes certain.[35]

CHAPTER SIX

Fear: The Primary Psychological Force

One thing is certain, that the problem of anxiety is a nodal point, linking up all kinds of most important questions; a riddle, of which the solution must cast a flood of light on our whole mental life.
— SIGMUND FREUD[1]

AVERSIVE VS. APPETITIVE LEARNING

Evolutionarily conserved inclination toward aversive (unpleasant) stimuli compared with appetitive (pleasant) ones has been documented in animals and humans.[2] Increased sensitivity to aversive stimuli, even if the probability of untoward outcomes is low, reduces the risk of underestimating safety and increases the odds of survival. This "better safe" than being correct attitude takes the upper hand and is likely conserved in the animal kingdom. One question echoes loudly in this context: Do humans do good things to pursue pleasure or avoid displeasure? For example, if one works to earn income, is it because of the motivation to be rewarded with money, which is a positive experience—pleasure—or to avoid the risk of poverty, a negative state? When people eat delicious food, the motivation is clearly to seek sensual pleasure rather than avoid the risk of starvation because people often eat multiple times a day when there is no risk of starvation, anxiety of nutritional deficiency, or threat to existence. Even in this situation, the thought of missing a delicious dish, perhaps unconsciously, may also influence someone to eat the food. In fact, it is hard to determine the proportion of the negative state (thought of missing food) and positive state (seeking pleasure) in eating delicious food, although the pleasure-seeking factor appears to be the dominant and primary factor. While this is the typical example of pleasure-seeking behavior, the proportion becomes more complex in other instances. When a student prepares for an examination, what is the dominant or primary driving factor? Is it the anxiety of a low grade in the examination or the pleasure of success? Or are they equal? We may believe the pleasure or reward of gain and success motivates people. However, a literature review of emotions and human behavior suggests that negative emotions are stronger than positive ones.[3] Marcus and MacKuen state the following: "The idea of threat as an attention-getting device makes common sense. Hit it over the head with a two-by-four, and you can get the attention of even a mule. Nothing focuses the mind so well as the prospect of one's own hanging."[4]

Given that the importance of anxiety is related to motivating living creatures, a brief discussion of motivation is warranted here. Essentially, motivation refers to the force that drives organisms to act. Motivation leads to initiation, continuation, and, sometimes, termination of the action. Motivation does not represent a unitary mental process. It is indeed an end phenomenon of several competing mental and physical phenomena such as urge, reason, sensory experiences, and possibly unconscious content. Factors influencing motivation can be internal, like desire for sensation, or external forces, namely threats or rewards.

The *content theory* of motivation deals with the internal needs of individuals as the determining factors. For Freud, the most prominent motivating force was unconscious drives. Abraham Maslow posited that a hierarchy of needs operates in humans in the following order: (a) physiological needs, which are the most basic, consisting of food, water, and other essential needs for survival; (b) security needs relating to safety, shelter, and emotional needs to be free from distress; (c) needs to belong, a higher need than a basic need, and represents the desire for friendship, love, and acceptance; (d) esteem needs relating to obtaining respect; and (e) the highest-level need for self-actualization, which represents achieving one's highest potential. According to Maslow's hierarchy, if needs are unmet, they motivate individuals, and lower-level needs are to be met before higher-level needs become motivational. Arguably, unmet needs may generate pressure and thus act as motivational.

In contrast to the need-based theories, the process theories of motivation put forward conscious decision-making processes as the motivating force. According to these theories, people work with the expectation that it will lead to outcomes they value (expectancy theory). The *equity theory* presents the perceived fairness of rewards of one's action relative to others. People see equity when they perceive that the ratio of efforts to rewards is the same for them as for others. Individuals will be motivated to reduce perceived inequity. According to *goal-setting* theory, specific and set goals influence motivation. Reinforcement theory posits that specific outcomes, called reinforcers, increase the odds of repeating the same behavior that resulted in reinforcers. The motivating factor here is the outcome of behavior, and learning is involved in this process.

REASON AND PASSION

According to Freud, discipline-inspired fears triumph over sex, aggression, and other biological forces. Intellectual faculties are regarded as more evolved characteristics of humankind, whereas emotions are treated as representatives of the continued inheritance of remnants of the animal brain. Passion is something to be mastered; the reason is to be cherished. While reason is indeed the signature of creative, surviving, and successful men, this view does not accommodate the role of emotions in human existence. Emotions are the value system of the mind. Romanticism broadly emerged as a reaction to rationalism, empiricism, and the Age of Enlightenment. The Romanticism movement focused on emotions, but as Solomon argues, it has not changed the "myth of passion"; instead, it has shifted priorities.[5]

Emotions and behavior are motivational, seeking either tension reduction or sensation. Human behavior or decision is a product of the interplay between these two motivational forces. It is argued that tension-reduction motivation is fundamental and more powerful than the motivation for sensual pleasure.[6] For Hobbes, the most determining force of human conduct is self-interest, and the strongest influence on self-interest is fear.* Fear is related to the preservation of the self. Other emotions, such as love and anger, typically develop in social contexts.

Almost all theories of personality include traits that have a common factor: anxiety. Various theories present it in labels such as neuroticism, harm avoidance, and behavioral inhibition.[7] LeDoux proposes two brain circuits of fear and anxiety: one deals with the feeling of fear, and the other is related to signals that can trigger defensive behaviors in the face of danger. The signals can also lead to the feeling of fear. He enumerates examples for this distinction: during food scarcity, signals of low energy can trigger fear of starvation; high altitude and low temperature produce signals that can induce fear of freezing and death. The brain circuits responsible for such signals are called defensive survival circuits. These circuits result in behaviors that help organisms survive. They are motivational but implicit and outside conscious awareness.

Dominance of Fear

Fear is capable of seizing humans.[†]

In general, emotional reactions are instantaneous, whereas intellectual evaluations are unrushed. Fear is capable of disrupting cognitive evaluation and shifting attention to its source. When we see a snake, attention unmistakably flows to the creature, the venom that can threaten life; everything else, including the beauty of the snake, becomes secondary. When we see lightning, what would be instantaneous is a feeling of fear or the physiological reactions of fear rather than the stunning beauty of branching lights.

Some emotions operate in antagonism. Fear conquers love and happiness; the physical manifestations of the latter two are less evident. Fear has the potential to virtually paralyze the organism and, hence, may

---

* According to Hobbes, when threatened by a conqueror, people covenant for protection by promising obedience. These are equally legitimate ways of establishing sovereignty, and their underlying motivation is the same—namely fear—whether of one's fellows or of a conqueror (*Stanford Encyclopedia of Philosophy*).
† Brutus says to the ghost of Caesar, "That makes my blood cold, and my hair to stare."

be considered the strongest emotion. It is also the primary emotion, given that it is ubiquitous, and all other emotions, manifestations of all instincts, depend on the strength of fear. Ralph Adolph proposes that fear is the central state of an organism and functional in that it causes adaptive behaviors to avoid or cope with threats.[8]

Operation of fear is not always with conscious awareness. A significant majority of human decisions are made based on unconscious processing.[9] Fear responses have been described in infants and adult subjects without conscious recognition. When the hidden memories (implicit memories) influence reflex actions in response to dangers, then fear response becomes an unconscious process. Like implicit or non-declarative memory, this is known as implicit, inherent, or non-declarative fear. James Gibson posited affordance perception as the basis of human actions. As mentioned in chapter 2, affordances are clues in the environment that indicate whether actions are possible according to one's resources. However, later research has shown that fear influenced perception and estimates of environmental measures. The theory of embodied perception states that emotions lead to changes in perceptual estimates and, hence, thought processes.

Anxiety is a perpetual phenomenon. No one escapes from its bitterness. It is a permanent condition, a lasting background emotion.[10] It is triggered and maintained by uncertainty and uncontrollability. It operates as a force driving organisms to take action. *Emotions* are transient and time-bound feeling states directed at a specific state of affairs.[11] In contrast, the mood is a sustained emotional tone typically lasting for days and weeks. Vazrad and Kurth argue that anxiety has a mood component without a specific target, a situation, or an object.[12] It is this kind of anxiety that is of interest to us. Given its constant operation, sustained anxiety acts as a dominant motivating force.

FEAR AND ANXIETY: THE ADAPTIVE SYSTEM

Decades ago, Mowrer described two types of reactions in response to threats.[13] One is voluntary and conscious behavior of avoidance of danger. The second is involuntary physical manifestations such as trembling, rapid breathing, palpitations, and similar reactions, which may occur without conscious control. The avoidant behavior is mediated by the actions of the brain on skeletal muscle, initiating a flight reaction and securing a safe haven. In contrast, involuntary autonomous reactions serve the avoidance behavior by enhancing the supply of oxygen and nutrients. Noradrenaline, which is activated during anxiety, is a powerful stimulant of heart and blood supply as well as attention. These two systems operate in coordination. Mowrer considers fear reaction as a result of learning and reflection on problem-solving. The behavior of avoidance is a problem-solving strategy originating from a drive, an innate instinct to remain at ease. Once the problem-solving avoidant behavior has achieved the result, which is safety and enhanced survival, the organism adopts the same strategy when threats occur in the future. Each time it succeeds, such behavior is strengthened. Avoidance, the central feature of behavior in anxiety, is thus reinforced and perpetuated.

When fear leads to flight, it is *reactive adaptation* because the fear gears the organism to develop a flight reaction following exposure to the threat. The second type of adaptation is an *inhibitory adaptation*, which happens when anticipated fear or anxiety stops an approaching action toward danger. Gray proposed a system that responds to dangers by stopping activities and increasing arousal and attention to the environment.[14] This is called the behavioral inhibition system (BIS). The proposal of BIS was based on empirical findings on the effects of antianxiety medications on animals and humans. During *reactive adaptation*, fear initiates action, but in *inhibitory adaptation*, anxiety stops action that may lead to injuries or threats to existence. In the case of *an inhibitory adaptation*, there is no reactive retreat following threatening events. Here anxiety is the psychological driving force that pressures and stops the organism from approaching dangers and hence serves the adaptive inhibitory functions of anxiety. This pressure causes tenseness inside and gets transformed into an operative force that stops the organism and thus helps the avoidance of danger. There is a third type of adaptive response, which is, in fact, a variant of reactive adaptation: *motivational reactive adaptation*. *Motivational reactive adaptation* is hypothesized to occur in reaction to a threat that manifests as a perceived deficit. For instance, when the food supply is short, individuals become anxious about starvation and then become motivated to seek food. Students may acquire the motivation to learn further upon their perception of inadequate preparation for an examination and subsequent development of anxiety. These are different from *reactive adaptation* proper in that in *motivational reactive adaptation*, individuals take actions to achieve positive outcomes and creativity, for example, to improve performance. In *reactive adaptation*, the proper action is to flee from danger, not necessarily with creative action.

Pain, acting as a signal of harm, can cause awareness of the threat and consequently motivate people to seek medical help. Denial of chest pain as a symptom of serious illness may lead to catastrophic outcomes if it is from a heart attack. Seeking medical help out of anxiety is affirmative action. While inhibitory and reactive adaptive systems are primarily concerned with avoiding immediate dangers and safety, *motivational reactive adaptation* is usually responsible for dealing with distant dangers by achievements rather than avoidance. *Motivational reactive adaptation* thus contributes to safety and welfare.

The adaptive systems mentioned herein operate across all levels of consciousness and unconsciousness. A vast amount of research has shown, as described in chapter 4, that people may exhibit fear reactions without conscious awareness of fear. An experiment showed that healthy subjects participating in gambling had autonomous arousal signs (e.g., palpitation) before they were aware of risky choices.[15] Although attractive, they did not choose risky offers after experiencing losses. Also, they demonstrated conscious reasoning that followed unconscious autonomous arousals. In contrast, patients who had damage to the ventromedial prefrontal cortex did not experience autonomous arousal nor show avoidance of risky choices. Autonomous arousal, such as skin conductance changes, was a proxy indicator of fear. It was inferred that patients with prefrontal damage could not experience fear. Only a tiny proportion of knowledge stored in the brain becomes available to consciousness. However, knowledge can be operative without conscious awareness. Unconscious knowledge may manifest in task performance. Previous emotional experiences from comparable situations could influence unconscious non-declarative knowledge, which preceded conscious reasoning. Unconscious knowledge of threat, uncertainty, or a negative outcome is hypothesized to cause fear without conscious awareness. It is also possible that unconscious knowledge can generate unconscious fear in a manner that conscious knowledge leads to conscious anxiety. We can reasonably hypothesize that unconscious fear reactions in the face of danger represent the adaptive fear systems operating without conscious recognition. Such an unconscious fear can be the operating drive in all types of adaptive systems: reactive, inhibitory, and motivational. To summarize, fear, as a dominant psychological force, at varying levels of consciousness, acts incessantly in maintaining safety and contributes to welfare and survival. Enduring and implicit anxiety manifests as vigilance, physiological arousal, and planning for defense. Implicit and unconscious memories help humans to operate day-to-day events and ensure survival through actions from moment to moment.

In the same way, inherent anxiety alerts us constantly against dangers. Every danger may not be consciously recognized, implying the role of unconscious anxiety in dealing with dangers outside conscious awareness. Hypotheses about unconscious operations were discussed elsewhere.[16]

The adaptive reactions at an unconscious level are pervasive and constant across all activities of life. Fear and anxiety thus incessantly regulate our actions and contribute to safety and welfare. Consistent with this hypothesis, neuroimaging data, although with inherent limitations, suggest that the bed nucleus of stria terminalis—the brain region associated with vigilance—showed sustained activation anticipating threat.[17]

The bed nucleus of stria terminalis is responsible for sustained attention, otherwise known as vigilance, given that its activity is associated with unpredictability. Unpredictability and uncertainty imply timeless activity. It can, therefore, be further hypothesized that the basal activity of the bed nucleus of stria terminalis is associated with sustained baseline anxiety that is constantly present, although in varying degrees and at levels of consciousness. Also, the activity of the bed nucleus of stria terminalis shows episodic and transient bursts, possibly in response to changing degrees of threat.

Chapter Seven

Benefits of Anxiety

Fear has functional and preparatory roles in dealing with future threats. These normative and protective aspects of fear lead to the concept of *functional fear*.[1] Unlike the traditional view of anxiety, its benefits are increasingly recognized in the recent past.[2] These benefits are broadly two: (1) survival and safety; and (2) motivating behavior. Common to both is a learning component in anxiety. Anxious avoidance of dangers and anxiety-induced motivation represents learning from previous experiences registered in memory circuits. Learning from mistakes is critical for adaptive behavior.[3] A dangerous encounter not only makes an imprint but also creates ripples; such encounters make animals and humans sensitive to signals from the same or similar encounters in the future. By learning these signals, we can predict dangerous encounters from cues and avoid future encounters.[4]

People who worry may get motivated to seek solutions.* Empirical evidence, albeit limited, supports this hypothesis. Anxiety is a motivational force.[5] For example, let us consider a gap in our knowledge and uncertainty. This is perceived as a defect and anxiety-provoking. Anxiety is unpleasant and sometimes unbearable. One method to deal with this problematic uncertainty, doubts, and knowledge gap is to seek information.[6] In this scenario, anxiety was the original cause of knowledge-acquiring behavior. Anxiety acts as a signal for the need for an evidence-collecting behavior or

---

* From the time of Aristotle, it was held, as seen in the work of Hobbes, that fear has been the foremost element in motivation. Harry Stack Sullivan pointed out that fear creates a tension that motivates the sufferer to take remedial actions that may remove the danger or escape from them.

epistemic behavior as well as an enhanced thinking (cognitive) process to solve uncertainties and knowledge (epistemic) gaps.[7] Since anxiety makes the problematic uncertainty salient and channels cognitive activities to solve the problem, it becomes an adaptive emotion. Epistemic anxiety thus has value in the face of limited cognitive resources.

INSTRUMENTAL AND INTRINSIC VALUES OF ANXIETY

When anxiety mediates escape or avoidance reactions, it becomes instrumental for survival. The instrumental value of anxiety is well known. It prepares organisms to deal with threats in an adaptive manner. Does anxiety have intrinsic value? This is answered in the following terms: unpleasantness of anxiety, epistemological value, and virtuous disposition.

Like pain, anxiety is unpleasant. Still, both pain and anxiety have been preserved during the process of natural selection. How? Have they been insignificant accompaniments of other traits that survived? Have they been free riders? Pain and anxiety are essentially indicators, aversive warning signals caused by some encounters. For a moment, let us keep aside the nature of these encounters, and we will not consider whether they are threatening, dangerous, or rewarding at this stage. So, the focus is not on the nature of the event that provokes anxiety but on the features of anxiety itself.

The aversive nature of these warning signs implies that organisms will try to eliminate them. Unpleasant experiences are unwelcome—this is *a priori*. The best way to abolish anxiety is to eliminate the source of anxiety. Pragmatic control means we should not make a mistake in concluding that humans will make every effort to avoid or abort dangerous objects and situations. Now the question in front of us is whether such efforts are undertaken only because of an awareness of danger or because of the unpleasant experience of anxiety induced by danger. Or could it be a combination of both?

Let us further imagine an implausible situation: Instead of being an unpleasant experience, anxiety is a pleasant experience. In that case, it is hard to imagine that one would try to eliminate its source even though it is dangerous (e.g., people know smoking is dangerous, but it is experienced as stimulating, and many find it hard to quit. Speeding is unmistakably known as dangerous, but when the accompanying feeling is excitement, there is no prohibition for it). The consequences are catastrophic. If the nature of anxiety is pleasant and hence welcome, it will not serve the purpose of survival fitness. Therefore, the value of anxiety is its bitterness. In other words, the unpleasantness of anxiety has an intrinsic value.

Now, let us consider the nature of the stimulus causing anxiety, not the anxiety itself. Here, let us imagine that instead of a threatening one, a rewarding stimulus causes anxiety. In this situation, we stick to the real nature of anxiety, its unpleasantness. A person may still try to eliminate the rewarding stimulus because anxiety caused by it is unpleasant. To escape tormenting anxiety, the person must also avoid the rewarding or reassuring stimulus that would otherwise bring welfare. It should not take much effort to see that such a scenario is incompatible with existence. In reality, as always, the rewarding stimuli do not cause anxiety. It is always a threatening, dangerous stimulus that causes anxiety. So, in trying to eliminate anxiety, organisms also eliminate threats to their existence. Therefore, the intrinsic value of anxiety, its unpleasantness, becomes adaptive only when coupled with a dangerous stimulus. It is the nature of the source of anxiety—the threatening encounters—and the anxiety experience itself—its unpleasantness—that give anxiety its survival value. No wonder such a combination with advantage got selected in the process of evolution. This combination gives anxiety a perfect fit.

Let us also consider other impacts of threatening stimuli. Suppose threats produce pleasure or love. It is instinctive for organisms to cherish the source of pleasure and love. If threats induce pleasure and love, then it is a straightforward conclusion that such a scenario is incompatible with survival. After confronting a stimulus, it is only when a person experiences pain or anxiety that an attempt to eliminate the stimulus will be made, not upon feeling pleasure or love. In this situation, anxiety also serves the purpose of survival and adaptive function. Organisms constantly try to reduce or abolish anxiety, and in doing so, they bolster their survival chances.

As seen above, anxiety involves uncertainty as its core element. Uncertainty implies a lack of knowledge—an epistemic gap. In response to unpredictability, anxiety builds up, motivating focus on attention and vigilance to capture salient information of the situations. Subsequently, anxiety and emotions, in general, activate cognitive processes so that they are streamlined to relevant information and tasks at hand. Such a prioritized utilization of limited cognitive resources is expected to fill the epistemic gap, resulting in a favorable and hence adaptive cognitive outcome.

The most important benefit of anxiety is hypothesized as risk-mitigating or harm-avoiding decisions and actions. Risk aversion is a decision tendency to avoid choices that could bear undesirable outcomes in the future. People with pronounced anxiety are likely to show risk aversion, given that they are already preoccupied with adverse outcomes. While this hypothesis is intuitive, is there any empirical evidence? Studies have shown inconsistent results with no trend, suggesting a straightforward conclusion. Findings from two studies that assessed participants' responses to day-to-day life scenarios supported the above hypothesis that increased anxiety was associated with a preference for safe alternatives. However, these results could not be replicated in other samples.[8] Moreover, another study that investigated gambling decisions failed to establish a link between anxiety and risky decisions.[9] Pathological anxiety, on the other hand, was associated with a propensity to avoid risk, a finding that was replicated.[10] Pathological anxiety was associated with an aversion for risks but not losses compared with the normal control population.[11] These findings may imply that risk avoidance is proportionate to the degree of anxiety. It need not necessarily be pathological anxiety, however. In a nonclinical sample of university school students, trait anxiety was associated with a relatively low willingness to take risks across a range of behavioral situations. This association remained after adjusting for the effect of depression.[12]

Facilitative Anxiety

In contrast to the traditional notion of anxiety as an enemy of life and performance, recent empirical evidence suggests an adaptive function of anxiety. It has long been held that anxiety is negatively correlated with cognitive performance. While this is supported by a wealth of studies and empirical findings, the relationship between anxiety and cognitive performance is not linear or straightforward. For instance, self-evaluation of anxiety as threatening with a sense of a lack of control is associated with impaired performance, whereas appraisal of anxiety as challenging and facilitative was met with enhanced performance.[13]

It is well known that anxiety redirects attentional resources to threats. Consequently, attention and working memory for neutral stimuli are impaired by a high level of anxiety. However, memory encoded within a negative context (e.g., a threatening one) is better retrieved during high anxiety levels than low anxiety.[14]

In a study of 103 undergraduate students who were approaching an examination, it was found that appraisal of stress as motivating correlated with better academic performance in comparison with viewing stress as threatening.[15] In addition, such a positive correlation was more pronounced with a high level of anxiety than with a low level of anxiety—students who saw stress as facilitative experienced less emotional exhaustion. In analyzing the findings, the authors adjusted for other factors that could affect the results, such as the level of motivation and other emotions. These results were consistent with a previous study that observed a positive association between efficient performance and stress when stress was perceived as challenging more than threatening.[16] Another study found a positive correlation between anxiety and efficient workplace performance among financial managers with reasoning capacity. These results suggest that anxiety's benefits depend broadly on three factors. One is the evaluative meaning of the anxiety-provoking situation, the second is a sense of self-efficacy, and the third is a high level of intellectual skills. The sense of self-efficiency is characterized by the idea that increased effort can overcome a challenge.

A counterargument is that rather than anxiety, reward or success in performance acts as the source of motivation. People engage in daydreams and imagine successful outcomes with consequent anticipatory pleasure. These factors can motivate people to make extra efforts. These are rational arguments; pleasure is a motivating principle. Intuitively it is pleasure that is motivating, not negative emotions like anxiety. Even when we accept these arguments, they need not necessarily abolish the role of anxiety as a contributory factor to positive outcomes. We must be careful again in proposing how anxiety acts as a motivation. When we say

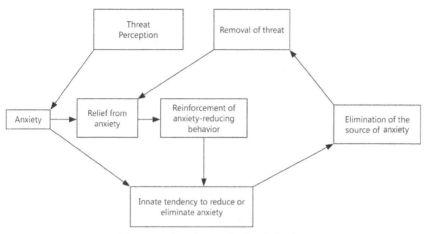

Threat and anxiety-reducing behavior

anxiety is the motivating factor, it is, in fact, a reduction or elimination of anxiety—the intended goal—which is the real motivator.

Desire or motivation to reduce tension is fundamental to the existence of organisms. Tension reduction is accomplished by eliminating or avoiding tension-creating objects or situations. Avoidance of dangers is the central feature of behavioral responses in anxiety. Anxiety is associated with arousal and vigilance.[17] The key benefit of anxiety is a powerful motivating force generated by its unpleasant and aversive feeling that eventually results in avoidance of danger.

We have seen three types of anxiety-related adaptive behaviors in the previous chapter: inhibitory, reactive, and motivational reactive adaptive mechanisms. The benefits of such adaptive systems include not only actions of safety but also outcomes with positive gains; for instance, anxiety about failure in an examination or competition may lead to enhanced effort and consequent success. Awareness of unpreparedness for examinations or competitive sports can prompt candidates to work hard and earn success.[18] In other words, anxiety is a motivating force bringing safety and welfare. This is consistent with a broad perspective of the utility of emotions as motivating forces.[19]

In a critical analysis of Pavlov's inferences, Mowrer argues that when a conditioned threat (the buzzer) elicits a conditioned behavior of avoidance, two processes are overlooked. One is learning the conditioned threat, and the other is problem-solving strategy. He, therefore, considers conditioned avoidant behavior as a problem-solving behavior driven by desires inherent in organisms. Hunger and thirst are primary drives that are the products of metabolisms in our body, whereas appetite and anxiety are secondary drives produced by conditioning. For Mowrer, organisms find solutions for both primary needs, which are biological, and secondary needs, which are emotional. Avoidance behavior is essentially a manifestation of an underlying need for peace of mind.

In a historical but surprisingly ignored experiment, Yerkes and Dodson observed learning in mice with increasing shock intensities.[20] When mice were trained for simple learning based on black-and-white discrimination, they avoided shock, and the rate of learning improved with the increasing intensity of the shock. However, when mice were trained for more difficult cues—black and gray instead of black and white—their learning rate improved until the moderate intensity of shock, not beyond that, and the learning was impaired with the highest intensity of the shock. The findings implied that for simple tasks, increasing stress may act as a motivating force and enhance performance. However, with complex tasks, optimal performance occurs with an intermediate stress level. The Yerkes-Dodson curve was incorrectly interpreted, and only monolithic curvilinear performance of the complex task performance was known in academic circles for a long time.[21] Later, Broadhurst and other authors replicated the findings in animal and human experiments.[22] Lewis et al. demonstrated that mild stress associated with examination preparation was associated with improved performance on the digit backward test, suggesting a positive effect of stress on the manipulative component of working memory.[23]

Subsequent research generated overwhelmingly diverse results, but a meta-analysis showed an overall negative association between anxiety and cognitive performance.[24] Reasons for heterogeneous results are worth considering. Reviews suggest that a mild level of stress facilitates cognitive functions such as memory when the tasks are simple.[25] A high level of stress or lasting stress was found to be detrimental to working memory function, cognitive flexibility, and decision-making, whereas a low level of intermittent stress enhanced performance in these domains. Also, the delay between exposure to stress and the timing of task performance appeared to determine the outcome: the immediate effect was negative, but a delay from four to 24 hours improved the performance.[26] In the same vein, Potvin et al. found that anxiety positively correlated with language fluency and general cognitive functioning when confounders such as age, education, depressive symptoms, subjective health, and chronic diseases were adjusted. The beneficial effects on cognition were seen even with high and moderate anxiety.[27]

The relationship between anxiety and cognitive performance can sometimes cause spiraling deterioration. A high level of anxiety adversely affects cognitive function, which, in turn, may cause more anxiety than in the beginning. This sets a vicious circle. Eysenck and Calvo argued that the effect of anxiety on cognition, although mostly detrimental, is complex.[28] Essentially, anxiety distracts attention preferentially to threatening stimuli, often irrelevant ones, upon facing goal-directed tasks. However, in the presence of anxiety, additional resources are allocated to cognitive processes so that the final outcome is achieved with increased effort. Therefore, effectiveness or maximal output is not affected by anxiety as efficiency is. Efficiency is effectiveness divided by effort. Suppose a task is successfully completed with extra effort and mobilization of additional mental resources. In that case, the efficiency is said to be low compared with the successful completion of a task with less effort and resources. Anxiety can also affect effectiveness if the complexity of tasks is high with the requirement of working memory. Upon facing challenging situations such as examination, highly anxious individuals may show typical anxiety reactions with avoidant behavior; they may escape from the situation, perceiving examination as a threat. At the same time, they may worry about the consequences of avoidance and escape, viz., negative judgment by others, failure in academic progress, diminished self-esteem, and material losses. If they take an examination as a challenge, they proceed with increased effort. Such a compensatory mechanism prevents deterioration of their performance.

The above empirical finding is consistent with the known neurobiology of anxiety, as described in the early part of this book. Anxiety-provoking situations are associated with the release of noradrenaline in the brain.[29] Noradrenaline causes multiple physiological accompaniments of anxiety, for instance, palpitation, rapid breathing, and sweating. At the same time, noradrenaline plays a crucial role in arousal, alertness, and attention, enhancing memory and learning. Findings derived from brain scan studies showed that memory function is proportionate to the integrity of locus coeruleus function.[30]

ANXIETY AND INTELLIGENCE

The impact of anxiety on memory and other cognitive functions does not follow a universal rule; it depends on its intensity. There is no doubt that anxiety beyond a limit will adversely affect cognitive flexibility and decision-making.[31] Given that anxiety is related to anticipation of imagined threats and subsequent planning, some authors point out that anxiety and intelligence could be related.[32] This is based on a hypothetical construct as well as an empirical basis. The hypothesis is that survival is favored by a response to a false alarm (false positive) rather than the absence of a response to an actual threat (false negative). Empirical findings suggest a positive correlation between one of the measures of intelligence and worry in both clinical populations with generalized anxiety disorder[33] and people without anxiety disorders, for instance, financial service managers.[34] Notably, a positive correlation between improved performance and anxiety was seen among managers with pre-existing high cognitive ability indicated by a high score on intelligence tests.[35] In another study, a positive correlation was found in patients with generalized anxiety disorder, but in healthy control subjects, this relation was inverse.[36] The authors argue that anxiety and intelligence co-evolved. Later, Penney et al. reproduced similar findings in a nonclinical population of undergraduates and demonstrated that verbal intelligence was a positive predictor of worry and rumination.[37]

Empirical data suggests that in unfamiliar and novel situations, deliberative citizens become anxious, seeking more information, accommodating opposing views, and preparing for compromise.[38] Similarly, certainty-associated emotions are more related to the heuristic processing of information than uncertainty-associated emotions, such as anxiety, which are followed by systematic reasoning.[39] Experimentally induced anxiety in children resulted in a long time for decision-making but fewer errors compared with the performance prior to anxiety induction.[40] The motivating effect of anxiety on information-seeking behavior has been discussed elsewhere.

SELF-EVALUATION OF ANXIETY AND ANXIETY MOTIVATION

Upon perception of threats, several defense mechanisms will be activated and mobilized. Apart from the fear reaction, a subjective appraisal of one's own sustained emotion (called mood) is also part of the defensive reaction. The awareness of one's mood is called meta-mood.[41] In fact, this is more than awareness; it is self-reflective, evaluative, and judgmental (e.g., "There is no need for me to feel angry"). Regulation of emotions by cognitive processes may follow awareness of emotions. In this way, workers facing strict timelines identify their emotions of anxiety and utilize cognitive resources such as thinking about the consequences of failing deadlines to motivate themselves to complete the work on time. Strack et al. have demonstrated that the clarity of feelings is associated with favorable interaction between anxiety and academic performance.[42] The mediating factor helping positive interaction is motivation induced by anxiety. The following components measured anxiety motivation:

- Feeling anxious about a deadline helps to get the work done on time.
- Feeling anxious helps to focus on what one needs to improve upon.
- Feeling anxious about one's goals keeps the person focused on them.
- Feeling anxious in the past created motivation to achieve some important goals in life.

FEAR APPEALS

Fear appeals are persuasive messages emphasizing potential danger that may befall individuals if they do not act in accordance with the messages' recommendations.[43] These messages induce anxiety in recipients. Leventhal et al. studied the effect of fear-rousing communications on smoking behavior.[44] They found that high fear appeals induced the desire to quit smoking but did not affect smoking behavior. Receipt of the information on how to quit smoking did not bring a change in desire; instead, it led to a change in smoking behavior. Although participants who experienced high fear levels complied with the recommendations to stop smoking, they were reluctant to get an X-ray. These findings suggest that fear appeals combined with the correct information may result in both a desire to quit and smoking cessation. Fear appeals may be delivered to the audience with a message about the recipient's ability to act according to the recommendations. When the recipients get a message that they have the skills and capacity to fulfill the recommendation, they develop self-efficacy. Similarly, when they learn that the recommended actions will reduce the danger, they get a sense of response efficacy.[45] Fear appeals may have varying severity; for instance, a message "excess speed can lead to loss of license" has less severity than saying "excess speed can lead to death." Evidence suggests that the more severe the messages, the more effective they are.[46] A systematic review and meta-analysis of 127 studies involving 27,372 participants show that fear appeals are effective in bringing intended behaviors and attitudes.[47] Intriguingly, their effectiveness has a ceiling: beyond a level, they stop working, but they did not backfire. Messages with efficacy statements had more effect than those without efficacy statements, but messages without efficacy statements did not have a negative effect. Fear appeals that indicated a person's susceptibility ("your vehicle is not tested for safety and, therefore, you are in danger") were more effective than the messages without susceptibility statements.

Disulfiram was the first medication approved by the Food and Drug Administration (FDA) for disorders associated with excess alcohol consumption. Clinical studies demonstrated that when disulfiram was taken under supervision, more participants in this medication group remained abstinent from alcohol than in placebo.[48] Disulfiram works by inducing anxiety about an unpleasant reaction that occurs when the medication is taken concomitantly with alcohol. Such a reaction can be severe and potentially fatal. Knowledge of this unpleasant effect, its anticipation, and associated anxiety act as a deterrent for continued drinking. This suggests that fear of unpleasant and extreme adverse effects was powerful enough to avoid alcohol despite the craving for it. In controlled trials, disulfiram was superior to other medications that act by suppressing cravings, such as naltrexone and acamprosate. Of significance, subjects who took disulfiram reported lower levels of craving compared with naltrexone, which itself is an anti-craving medication. Whether fear of a disulfiram-alcohol reaction thwarted cravings for alcohol and motivation to drink is unknown. Regardless, these findings imply the role of fear in maintaining safe behavior.

The use of recreational substances is seen as a coping strategy to deal with high anxiety. Therefore, there is an association between morbid anxiety and increased levels of substance abuse in children.[49] Nonetheless, scrutiny of these results shows that the outcomes are not uniform; for instance, a high level of social and separation anxiety in adolescents is associated with reduced rates of substance abuse, whereas extreme anxiety, such as panic attacks, is associated with increased substance abuse. The effect of anxiety on risk-taking behavior may not be apparent in ordinary situations. Under stress, individuals with a high level of anxiety choose actions of low risk compared with those with a low level of anxiety.[50] These observations suggest that the effect of anxiety in risk mitigation is visible and relevant during a stressful situation.

In the past, a few studies suggested that fear was associated with negative outcomes, such as the termination of failing entrepreneurship and acquiring information that led to the rejection of opportunities for peace during conflicts. These studies also indicated that hope was associated with escalating commitment to the venture and acceptance of opportunities for peace.[51] Certain caveats are questioning these conclusions. First, fear and hope are not antithetical or mutually exclusive. As evident in the studies of fear appeals, a sense of self-efficacy, a cognitive schema that is related to hope, actually increases the effectiveness of fear appeals.[52] While fear is the product of underestimating a positive outcome and overestimating a negative outcome, such thinking does not automatically negate hope.

Eysenck suggests the mechanism of adaptive functions of anxiety. According to this model, a threat in the environment generates an alert signal. In response to this alert, individuals collect information about the threat. The information gathered triggers a prompt function—retrieval of threat information from long-term memory. A preparatory action follows this in anticipation of an aversive outcome. The preparatory action may prevent the untoward event or enhance coping. Moreover, with repeated worries, a process of habituation will occur, which will then lead to a reduction in the aversiveness of the anticipated outcome.[53] Vividness is known to influence risky judgments. Information about an accident with cognitive details, such as possible ways an accident occurred, had more impact on decisions than the mere provision of simple statistical data like probability estimates.[54] Along the same line, personal experiences of past aversive outcomes were associated with self-protective behavior.[55] Direct confrontation with threats may have a more powerful impact on future behavior than hearsay information.

Temperament Traits and Harm Avoidance

Temperament refers to the style of behavior in contrast to the motivational part (why) or its content (what). Temperament is thus how behavior manifests. Robert Cloninger developed four temperament traits: harm avoidance, novelty seeking, reward dependence, and persistence.[56] Harm avoidance reflects a heritable bias of aversion or inhibition of behavior in response to signals of punishment, pain, or frustration. It manifests as anxiety about the unknown, shyness, social inhibition, and passive of avoidance of danger. People with high harm avoidance worry in anticipation, take a cautious approach, and adopt careful planning. These traits are advantageous when hazards are likely. They are maladaptive when the probability of danger is low.

In experimental contexts, individuals with a high level of anxiety to the extent of anxiety disorders have shown less risky choices when faced with gambling tasks without an opportunity to learn from prior experiences.[57] They demonstrated a risk-avoiding tendency even after a gain. They were less happy after a gain and less sad after a loss compared with the comparison group without anxiety disorders. Similar findings were also observed in nonclinical samples without anxiety disorders. Data from university students suggested that anxiety was associated with a heightened perception of a negative outcome and a low willingness to make risky decisions.[58] Such an association remained after depression was adjusted for. However, some studies showed contradictory results.[59] The heterogeneity of findings is explained by the intensity of ambiguity of the negative outcome, which is known to mediate the association between anxiety and less risk-taking behavior.[60] These findings show that anxiety acts as a deterrent factor against risk.

Wohl and Branscombe proposed that groups develop an aversive group-based emotional response upon facing the threat of group extinction. This is called collective angst.[61] Collective angst was found to be associated with the strengthening of the ties among the in-group members. A common threat that groups face may result in behavioral tendencies such as donating to organizations that serve the in-group, affiliating with fellow in-group members, and teaching children about the in-group's history and culture. Social studies of election campaigns have shown that anxiety stimulated attention toward the campaign, information processing, and political learning.[62] Enthusiasm, on the other hand, stimulated involvement in political campaigns, not learning. Moreover, with anxiety, people showed a reduced tendency to rely on habitual responses.

Chapter Eight

Role of Fear in Human Life and in Civil Society: Consequences of Fearlessness

I have come to believe that anxiety accompanies intellectual activity as its shadow and that the more we know of the nature of anxiety, the more we will know of intellect.

— H. S. Liddell[1]

Once upon a time, two men lived as close friends. One was brave as a warrior, and the other was a worrier. The brave man traveled across the globe and enjoyed expeditions, whereas the worrier mostly remained reclusive. From time to time, the brave man encouraged the worrier to go out and explore the world. Peer pressure and social learning worked. Initially a harm-avoidant person, the worrier realized that he missed many attractions in the world and gradually changed his lifestyle to become a globetrotter but never like his companion adventurer. One day, they decided to go together to see a waterfall. Wielded with confidence from previous experiences, the brave man wanted to enjoy the stunning view from the waterfall's edge. He jumped to the shallow water on the top, not far from the edge. The worrier was afraid to get into the water, but the brave man reassured him. He stepped into the water, and they both moved toward the edge. However, like a chain that wrapped and pulled from behind, the fear of falling from the top of the waterfall stopped the worrier. The brave man did not persuade the worrier this time, and heedless of the worrier's hesitancy, he proceeded toward the edge. He could see the vast earth from the top of the waterfall and became excited. He derived pleasure from numerous such explorations in life. The worrier, while being fearful, ruminated over the lost opportunities of the past and momentarily felt envious of the brave man who was enjoying the breathtaking view from the very edge. The worrier remembered the Shakespearean words, "a coward dies many times before his death." The valiant wanted to see the bottom of the waterfall. The rock that could prevent someone from going over the edge was slippery. It failed to stop the brave man from falling.

In Kurth's view, a social organization does not evolve spontaneously; it needs to be cultivated and policed.[2] The basic units of social cohesion originate from regard for others' needs. What does motivate people to show respect for others? A consensual answer is a social value system—respect and reciprocity are regarded as values, in other words, desirable goals. We have seen that emotions constitute our value system. Individuals in every society strive for recognition and respect from others. This creates pressure to equally respect and reward others because a lack of mutual respect and reward may be perceived as a threat of denial of the same to oneself. Some argue that anxiety is required to infuse self-discipline in certain behavioral situations.[3] This view is connected to the observation that anxiety strongly influences thoughts and behavior. In people with brain damage in the frontal lobes, characteristic personality and behavioral features have been described.[4] One subtype lacked emotions, social withdrawal, poor planning, indecisiveness, and poor judgment. Anxiety and depression were low in the subtype.

Without constant anxiety, humans will instantaneously engage in dangerous and life-threatening behavior. Ignoring warning signs of heart attack and an extreme weather event are signs of fearlessness and can be fatal. Loewenstein argues that it is insufficient fear that accounts for the indifference toward climate change.[5] Fear operates in war and stock markets, but when it comes to climate change, there is a collective deficiency of fear.

We have seen a few examples of the consequences of fearlessness: the medical student who took medication to abolish anxiety and the man who approached the edge of a waterfall. Let us go one step further and examine a mental state called *mania*. Mania is a morbid mental state, part of a mental disorder commonly known as a bipolar mood disorder. Mania is characterized by an elevated state of mind associated with increased psychological and physical activity. It is a state of increased arousal. In the classic form of mania, affected individuals experience excess happiness—euphoria—whereas anger, irritability, or even dysphoria occurs in the irritable, paranoid form of mania. *Delirious mania* is an extreme and potentially lethal type in which affected individuals become disorganized and exhausted from strenuous physical activities.

Several other features accompany mania: enhanced positive thinking, such as grandiosity, and expansive ideas, such as buying a large property. Sometimes, associated beliefs progress to delusional nature. Anxiety is conspicuously absent in mania, possibly drowned in morbid euphoria and inflated self-esteem. Affected individuals typically contemplate no regard for the consequences of their actions. Manis is notoriously known for reckless behavior that can invite catastrophic outcomes. It is a prototype syndrome showing the dangerous consequences of fearlessness.

When fear evolved in nature, its advantages—preparing for a defensive reaction against dangers—applied to threats that existed in ancient society. They included predating animals, natural forces, and environmental hazards. Although the original ones still exist, the threats in the modern world have evolved. For instance, motor vehicle and industrial accidents contribute heavily to human loss, but no innate or inherited fear reactions to these objects or situations exist. In these situations, fear develops when these accidents involve stimuli provoking inborn fear, such as loud noise or fire. This naturally questions the adaptive value of fear in the modern world.

In this context, the differences between fear and anxiety are critical. As described in the first two chapters, learned and evolved fear is anxiety. Anxiety essentially arises from the unknown and uncertain future. We have every reason in front of us to presume that uncertainty has occupied consciousness throughout human evolution. This implies that anxiety, as it is related to a sense of uncertainty, is timeless. Therefore, anxiety is as relevant in the modern world as it was in the ancient world. It is different from primitive, autonomous, and instantaneous fear reactions. Anxiety originates from symbols of modern life, words people use, and financial and social insecurity, unlike physical and environmental threats that cause fear, which can sometimes be detached from thinking. An organized modern society would be impossible without anxiety. Regulations and laws enforced by governments are in response to the anticipated untoward outcomes. We have already seen that emotions are the motivating factors for decisions and actions. Humans need a driving force to make decisions and then act. This driving force is motivation. Emotions like love motivate people to do things that please them.

On the other hand, fear is the emotion when people are motivated to do things that they do not like to do. No emotion other than anxiety motivates men to do unpleasant things such as obeying laws, ceasing smoking, and paying taxes. For instance, traffic rules are formed by authorities because of the anxiety related to traffic accidents. Motorists obey them for fear of infringement notices and possible loss of license. Citizens obey laws as they are fearful of sanctions if they breach laws. Anxiety is the only mental phenomenon that prompts men to do ego-dystonic acts. Here, we see an unpleasant emotion motivates people to do unpleasant things. This indicates one of humanity's greatest mysteries because such an unpleasant emotion motivates people to do unpleasant things across species—the puzzle multiplies when unpleasantness is related to a survival advantage.

The Risk Society, a concept proposed by Ulrich Beck and Anthony Giddens, depicts a social order characterized by socially constructed hazards such as air pollution, radiological hazards, and food contamination.[6] Men live in a world that is increasingly facing such dangers. Are people becoming more anxious in recent times? Twenge published two meta-analyses showing increasing anxiety levels among Americans over the past decades. American children in the 1980s experienced more anxiety than reported by children in the 1950s.[7] These findings were not supported by a recent meta-analysis involving European populations, which did not show increased anxiety levels over time.[8]

Jackson and Everts describe anxiety at a social level and how anxiety mobilizes associations and social institutions in response to perceived dangers.[9] In line with Freud's arguments that emotions in a group are contagious, Brennan suggests that physical and social environments facilitate the transmission of anxiety and depression among individuals.[10] Social issues with anxiety lead to the concept of social risk, which then brings the dimension of moral norms into it. Jackson and Everts argue that social anxiety can take massive scales and expand compared to personal anxiety. Food contamination scares expressed by the public may prompt supermarkets to withdraw contaminated food items.

Fearlessness is regarded as central to the development of psychopathy.[11] Conscience and internalized regulators of behavior have been linked to prosocial behavior. Internalization of maternal instructions, including prohibitions, was taken as one measure in studies of children that assessed the relationship between fear and conscience. Findings implied that fearful children might surpass fearless children as far as conscience is concerned during preschool.[12] Maternal discipline promoted conscience in fearful children, and with secure attachment, fearless children also developed conscience, but they still showed some antisocial responses. Waller et al. argue that fearlessness is associated with low arousal toward distress in others, resulting in impaired learning about outcomes of harmful behavior with a predisposition to callousness. Fearlessness was associated with callous-unemotional behavior at 12 years when children received low positive parenting, but this outcome was mitigated with a high level of positive parenting.[13] Taken together, these studies suggest that secure attachment and positive parenting reduce the impact of fearlessness.

Several studies have shown that individuals with antisocial personality traits have a diminished capacity to experience fear.[14] In his famous book *The Mask of Sanity*, the American psychiatrist Hervey Milton Cleckley describes features of sociopathy, the absence of nervousness, as one among them.[15] Lack of fear, it is argued, is associated with profound disregard for future consequences.[16] In some instances, fearlessness is associated with high prosocial risk-taking behavior, if not necessarily antisocial risk-taking.[17] In a follow-up study, Gao et al. demonstrated that poor fear response at three years was associated with an increased incidence of crimes at the age of 23. The fear response was assessed by electrodermal measurements.[18] Fearlessness and stimulus-seeking behavior predicted aggressive behavior at 11 years in male and female children, but the relationship between fearlessness and aggression was mediated by height.[19]

The "fear deficit" in psychopathy has been revisited in the past decade.[20] *Fearlessness* is a broad term. Specifically, it may encompass physiological and psychological features such as impaired threat sensitivity, low anxiety, and shallow emotional experiences.[21] The complicating factor is a distinction between unconscious and reflective fear reaction and conscious and contemplative experiential fear, as LeDoux described.[22] It is suggested that rather than general *fearlessness*, individuals with psychopathy have reduced threat detection sensitivity and diminished response to threats.

Another challenge in developing conclusions about fearlessness in psychopathy is the heterogeneity of neuroimaging findings, particularly those related to the amygdala, the brain structure typically studied in relation to fear. Although an early study showed reduced amygdala activity, it was contradicted by recent findings.[23] Nonetheless, the amygdala volume was reduced in psychopathy, and experimental findings suggest impaired conscious feelings of fear in psychopathy.[24] Adding to inconsistencies, Lamoureux and Glenn demonstrated that individuals with psychopathic traits could feel fear and show threat sensitivity.[25] Discrepancies in results could be due to limited reliability from recollection and reporting biases from participants, time of assessments, and variance within the construct of psychopathy. In this regard, a longitudinal study showed that reduced amygdala volume in subjects with psychopathy predicted future risk of violence.[26]

Variance within psychopathy has generated an approach that views psychopathy with different subtypes rather than as a unitary syndrome.[27] Karpman differentiated two types: primary and secondary; the former was characterized by interpersonal charm, selfishness, deceitfulness, and manipulation, as well as a heritable emotional deficit described as callousness, low anxiety experiences, and a lack of empathy.[28] Also, Hare and Neumann described two factors in psychopathy: factor 1 (F1) consisting of interpersonal (e.g., manipulative) and emotional (e.g., callousness) trait-based features, and factor 2 that includes lifestyle (e.g., need for stimulation) and antisocial features (e.g., poor behavior controls).[29] A recent review of broad literature suggests overall evidence for a low level of anxiety in primary psychopathy and F1.[30] This review has identified a methodological issue; conceptual differences between fear and anxiety are not addressed adequately in the studies of psychopathy. Such a lack of differentiation between fear and anxiety may also explain inconsistent findings. A detailed discussion of fear and anxiety changes in psychopathy is beyond the scope of this book. However, an important aspect of anxiety must be mentioned in this context. Unlike fear, which develops after exposure to specific but predictable cues, anxiety develops after unpredictable context conditioning.[31] This anxiety is associated with behavior that seeks to avoid painful stimuli. In contrast to fear, the study of anxiety is, therefore, critical in psychopathy.

Skin electric conductivity, also known as electrodermal activity, varies as per the function of sweat glands, which, in turn, is controlled by the sympathetic nervous system. When the sympathetic nervous system is stimulated, the skin's electric conductivity is also increased. Decreased skin electric conductivity is associated with low anxiety and weak behavioral control.[32] In summary, an adequate level of sympathetic activity brought by adrenaline and noradrenaline was associated with anxiety and socially refined behavior. Poor sympathetic activation was associated with social disregard and impulsiveness. It could be possible that a lack of sufficient anxiety and impaired social behavior represents an underlying common defect: poorly developed sympathetic activation. In previous chapters, we have seen how the sympathetic system, especially adrenaline, contributes to anxiety.

Defective Fear

The opposite of fearfulness may not be fearlessness, but recklessness.
—V. Sacco[33]

The neural networks involved in vigilance are affected in temporal lobe epilepsy.[34] When vigilance is adversely affected, it may lead to impaired caution and subsequent dangerous decisions. In the same vein, sensation seeking, a personality construct rather than a behavior as such, poses risks at multiple levels: social, physical, and financial.[35] Novelty-seeking behavior may bring pleasure or peril depending on whether it is met with a new source of food or a predator. We can see that this behavior was selected during the evolution process as it was adaptive, at least in some circumstances, if not in other situations which could be otherwise dangerous. High sensation-seeking individuals face increased risk as they may engage in self-destructive behavior. Drug abuse and gambling are a few behaviors associated with novelty seeking. In other instances, novelty seeking is regarded as heroic and, as a personality trait, highly represented among firefighters, surgeons, pilots, and police. Given the inherent risk of novelty seeking, these professions naturally require high safety precautions.

A lack of fear of contracting diseases can be associated with several adverse outcomes. During the COVID-19 pandemic, preexisting anxiety about contamination was one factor associated with safety behavior.[36] The implication is that the absence of such anxiety may lead to behaviors that may facilitate the spread of the disease. Sedentary lifestyles are manifestations of fearlessness. When people are anxious about the impact of physical inactivity, smoking, and excess consumption of calories, fat, and alcohol, sedentary lifestyles give way to healthy ones, such as using a treadmill. Disregarding warning signs of serious diseases occurs in fearlessness; people ignore unexpected weight loss, chest pain, skin spots, fever, altered behavior and mood, and signs of suicidal risk because of a lack of anxiety about the probability of serious diseases and disorders that these signs may indicate.

Another problem is a lack of compliance with treatment. Medical advice is not sought, and medications are not adequately taken when people are fearless. The absence of fear was associated with poor adherence to hygiene and social distancing during the COVID-19 pandemic, factors that facilitate the spread of the infection.

Fear of primitive times was restricted to strangers, cliffs, and similar crude stimuli. How did fear evolve and get generalized to regulate social norms? Charlie Kurth argues that anxiety developed alongside fear, which helped to make social life more complex.[37] After delineating the differences between fear and anxiety, Kurth makes an important distinction: it is in behavior. Fear behavior is situation-specific, such as flight, whereas anxious behavior involves generalized risk reduction, such as avoidant behavior and information-seeking actions or epistemic behavior. Animal research has shown both risk-minimizing as well as knowledge-seeking behavior attitudes. This is evident in an established baboon colony when a male newcomer joins. The arrival of a new baboon will be met with uncertainty and vigilance. The members of the established colony became restless, and they tracked every move of the newcomer but simultaneously avoided confrontation. They learn about the new baboon. Given uncertainty and unpredictability regarding the immigrant male's strength and hence the outcome of a fight, the baboons of the existing colony tried to minimize the risk of a costly fight.

Arne Öhman proposed that fear originated from a dominance-submissive system, specifically aggression from the dominant member, which caused fear in the subordinate. Such fear should have served as an advantage to both the dominant and subordinates by avoiding an unpleasant interaction. In modern democratic societies, a dominant-submissive system gives way to systems with organizational rules. Anxiety that develops in the dominance-submissive system may also develop in the context of organizational rules and regulations. Such rules can be legitimate, and anxiety about the consequences of rule violation may facilitate organizational order. An organization may fall apart if group members lack anxiety about the consequences of rule violations. Kurth contends that fear is a *ballistic* psychological mechanism, meaning that the bond between fear-provoking stimulus and the corresponding fear reaction is unbreakable. Fear is also a flexible phenomenon in that fear gets generalized from the original crude threats, such as predators, to other threats in the broad environment.

Kurth also argues that a subordinator is expected to know what can trigger aggression from the dominant person in the hierarchy. The knowledge that would help to avoid aggression from the dominant member facilitates submission and compliance with social norms. In this context, facial reactions of fear in the subordinate will convey a message of submissiveness to the dominant. By avoiding aggression, which can be perceived as a form of punishment, fear provides an incentive. Compliance with the dominant hierarchy thus gets merits (in modern democratic systems, this may be replaced by compliance with rules and regulations of organizations or laws of the land broadly). In this way, fear plays a role in norm internalization, in this particular instance, respect for social dominance-based hierarchy. Fear under such circumstances is expected to have a survival advantage in that it helps individuals to avoid the cost of norm violations. The group members identify with each other when they show trustworthiness and compliance with the social norm. The norms of policing and punishing will have disadvantages, whereas anxiety, as Kurth points out, can reduce the cost of norm violation. The role of anxiety in social regulation is not a solo one, however.

Along with anxiety, compliance with social norms entails knowledge of the consequences of norm violation and strategies to reduce the costly consequences: the evaluative component of the cognitive process. Also, as societies evolve into more complex structures with expanding populations, rules and norms may become less clear and certain. Individuals perceive this sort of normative uncertainty and experience subsequent anxiety. Kurth calls this *practical anxiety*. This anxiety arises from uncertainty about what norms are to be followed and what are to be avoided, in other words, prescriptions and prohibitions. Practical anxiety is associated with unique cognitive schema, deliberations, epistemic behavior, and motivations. There is intense debate about whether compliance with norms or law is a consequence of fear of punishment or a sense of moral obligation to do the right thing. The answer is irrelevant in this context because the moral obligation to the right also arises from anxiety. Experimental findings have demonstrated that anxiety traits, particularly that of harm to others, correlated with moral concerns.[38]

Worry, as previously described, is a thinking process (cognitive activity) with a recurrent pattern and essentially a negative content, typically an untoward future outcome or event.[39] Tallis et al. studied the phenomenology of worry.[40] People cannot escape from their worries even when they wish. Worry is experienced in linguistic form rather than images and narratives with elaborate negative or unpleasant themes. People commonly worry at night before sleep about real-life problems rather than imagined or distant dangers. Most people reported that worry is a good daily experience in that it stimulates problem-solving thinking. There are contradictory findings, however.[41] Other studies have reported negative consequences of worry, such as avoidance of performance and emotional discomfort. These negative features of worry were associated with catastrophizing thinking and a high level of worry.

Public fear of crime has been popularly depicted as a character weakness adversely impacting the quality of life, particularly social interactions, and freedom. Empirical evidence showed that crimes such as robbery resulted in public fear of crimes, leading to diminished social interactions; people seek safe havens. Their movements become constrained. Sequentially, reduced social interactions reduce the prospect of further crimes. Liska and Warner call this a paradoxical process—fear of crime, as a reaction to crime, may serve the function of controlling crime.[42] These findings underscore the potential of fear in the genesis of vigilance and undertaking precautionary activities. The ultimate effect of fear is reduced crime and improved safety.

Another investigation has demonstrated that one-quarter of participants surveyed reported worry as a problem-solving strategy.[43] They were worried, and they took precautions. Subsequently, they felt safe. Furthermore, they revealed that neither worry nor precautions reduced the quality of their lives. It can be argued that fear in such circumstances causes a damaging retreat, and those who fear crimes become psychological victims of crime. Jackson and Gray, however, point out the other side of the picture; fear initiates a beneficial risk mitigation strategy.[44] Victimization experience can follow dysfunctional worry. A blanket disapproval of fear may inflict social harm by eliminating its beneficial effects, particularly in reducing crime. Stereotyping fear as a character weakness and social problem presents a skewed view of fear, burying its adaptive functions. Rather than promoting judgmental and value-based comments about fear and making assumptions about the quality of life, journalists, political leaders, and sociologists may focus on the contributions of fear to public safety. Fear and anxiety are unpleasant experiences in life. These stark realities imply that fear and anxiety are necessary ingredients for safety and welfare.

ANXIETY AND VALUE SYSTEM

People value moral norms.[45] Schwartz describes values as beliefs that are linked to emotions.[46] For example, independence is a value. When independence is threatened, people experience arousal and become desperate when they perceive helplessness to protest. Values are desirable goals (e.g., justice) that motivate people. Certain values represent the effects of underlying anxiety. Self-protective values are examples. *Conformity* is a social value that arises from self-restraint of actions that may hurt others or violate social expectations, norms, or laws. When anxious, people tend to avoid conflicts with norms and laws. This facilitates conformity. After all, the need to belong and the desire for interpersonal attachment form powerful and pervasive motivation, which is pivotal for human existence.[47] Separation can bring anxiety, and an awareness of a group's dissolution can threaten its members.[48] Horney identified social isolation as a source of anxiety, a view that found some support in the work of Craighead et al.—the imagination of social rejection was associated with physiological arousal.[49] Empirical research showed that shame and social anxiety were associated with submissiveness.

People want to identify themselves as moral persons.[50] Research demonstrated that reparatory moral acts, prosocial behavior, and less cheating followed the recollection of past immoral behavior.[51] Past moral transgressions produced a sense of incompleteness, which was then met with compensatory moral behavior. Such moral cleansing presumably arises from a threat to one's perceived moral integrity. Supporting these views, empirical data show that reminders of past immortal behaviors led to avoidance of clues that suggested social rejection. For instance, angry faces and social anxiety modulated this association, the greater the anxiety, the stronger the avoidance.

Moreover, socially anxious individuals avoided clues of approval, such as happy faces, because of the fear of evaluation by others. In such instances, anxiety has the potential to cause moral reparatory and compensatory actions, which serve as an adaptive response to secure one's place in a group and promote social acceptance.[52] In other words, anxiety facilitates morality and consequent social conformity.

As demonstrated in experiments, a possible lack of fear was associated with risky choices.[53] It can also be argued that a lack of anxiety does not necessarily lead to disadvantageous choices; risky decisions may bring profit in return, for instance, investing money in shares and equities.[54] Therefore, the benefits of anxiety and adverse consequences of a lack of anxiety are contingent on risk in each situation. When all other factors are equal, the presence of anxiety can be decisive.

Anxiety and Morality

> *Fear is the mother of morals.*
> —Friedrich Nietzsche[55]

Morality has two broad definitions: descriptive and normative. Descriptively, morality refers to specific codes of conduct accepted by a society or by an individual for one's behavior. Normatively, morality is the code of conduct that, given specified conditions, would be put forward by all rational people. Koleva et al. point out that morality is social at its very core, motivated by social concerns of how one should relate to others.[56] As part of morality, people suppress selfishness and try to promote social cohesion. While anxiety within a relationship predicted concerns for moral themes such as fairness and impurity, callousness was associated with weak moral concerns.[57] It is worthwhile to note that individuals with both anxious and avoidant attachment styles show utilitarian moral concerns. However, Robinson et al. argue that the sources of such concerns differed between groups.[58] Avoidant people who hardly acknowledge distress expressed by others show utilitarian options out of a lack of concern for sacrificing an individual.

In contrast, anxious individuals do so from their aspiration for social approval. In other words, the utilitarian concerns among highly anxious individuals originated from their need to belong to a group.[59] Avoidant people show less empathy and concern for individuals who make sacrifices, possibly explained by their mistrust in relations.

Various mechanistic theories have been offered to explain moral concerns seen in people with a high level of anxiety. Anxiously attached individuals seek reassurance and approval and try to remain connected with others.[60] Given that anxiety essentially involves uncertainty, it promotes a strong need to belong and motivates efforts to gain the approval of others. Given that anxiety essentially involves uncertainty, it promotes a strong need to belong and motivates efforts to gain the approval of others. Additionally, anxious individuals show great compliance with requests from others because of the worry that partners will lose interest in them if noncompliant.[61] Extending this to a group, anxious individuals try to conform to a group to get acceptance. This may explain utilitarian moral judgment seen in people with a high level of anxiety.

From the above findings and implications, moral standards in anxiety states fundamentally arise from self-centered interests, such as the need for social validation rather than altruism. Findings support the argument that anxious people help people show volunteerism out of their insecurity within the relationships.[62] Also, anxious people offer help when the victims are identified or when they have knowledge about victims.[63] Such prosocial behavior was observed in less strenuous and less aversive situations.

Taken largely, a subset of moral and prosocial behaviors may be explained by anxiety rather than true altruism. Anxiety thus contributes to social relations, conformity to groups, and validation for oneself. An enigmatic aspect of this association is the opposing aesthetics of anxiety and morality. Anxiety is unpleasant and often regarded as a poor quality with a negative connotation. Morality, on the other hand, is a cherished concept with a positive light. Considering anxiety as the root mechanism of morality, at least in certain instances, can be considered provocative.

In shaping morality, fear of social disapproval is critical in that it inhibits the primitive instincts of individuals, which can potentially be socially disadvantageous and thereby indirectly facilitates the expression of a value system and moral conscientiousness. Civil obedience and law-abiding behavior essentially originate fear of incarceration or fines. Tillich argued that anxiety is a reaction to the ever-present.

INTIMATE RELATIONSHIP AND ANXIETY

Although a high level of anxiety is associated with an attachment style that is overprotective and intrusive, it was also found that caregiver anxiety was associated with instrumental support in times of high need.[64] Anxious individuals did not dismiss their partners' needs. In an experimental setting, highly anxious individuals showed better empathic accuracy in inferring their partner's thoughts or feelings than less anxious individuals.[65] Anxious individuals use strategies such as hyperactivating the attachment system by anticipating the worst outcomes, exaggerating cues of relationship threats, and showing vigilance. This can be a painful experience because these individuals may be exposed to the thoughts and feelings of their partners that they fear the most.[66] Empirical data suggest that in attachment systems, highly anxious individuals are ready to sacrifice for their partners. However, they were worried about reciprocation. They perceived a lack of reciprocation as having consequences for the relationship. Moreover, findings implied that once they received help, they would be eager to reciprocate.[67]

Novelty Seeking

A description of temperament has been given in the previous chapter. One is novelty seeking, which refers to a heritable bias indicating an affinity toward novelties. It manifests as appetitive behavior or activation of behavior toward signals of reward and avoidance of signals of punishment. It is called novelty seeking because the fundamental feature is exploratory approach behavior toward rewards. Novelty seeking can be adaptive in that it involves enthusiastic exploration of new possibilities or information potentially leading to discoveries. Exploring unchartered territories may be helpful in times of famine as well as in developing new medicines during a pandemic. Novelty seeking may identify new opportunities and can be adaptive. For instance, finding a new shelter can save a life while facing a predator. For Darwin, it is human nature to value novelty, however slight it is. It is shown that anxiety may stimulate novelty seeking in certain circumstances and decrease in other situations.

There is no consistent relationship between anxiety and novelty-seeking temperament.[68] However, empirical findings mostly suggest that they are negatively correlated, especially in situations that involve physical danger.[69] This is consistent with a marginal but nonsignificant negative correlation between novelty seeking, the severity of social anxiety disorder and obsessive-compulsive disorder, and reduced anxiety level in subjects with greater novelty seeking.[70]

Novelty seeking as a temperament trait is characterized by impulsiveness, extravagance in response to rewards, and avoidance of frustration. The maladaptive part of novelty seeking includes impulsivity, recklessness, susceptibility to boredom, anger outbursts, and fickle relationships. Sensation-seeking behavior is associated with recklessness, such as dangerous automobile driving, sex without contraception, alcohol and drug use, vandalism, and theft.[71] These findings indicate that a low level of anxiety and inherently high novelty-seeking behavior may be associated with the above maladaptive behaviors.

Adaptation originates from a patchwork of evolved gains, not in foresight, but in hindsight. Fear is central to forming a civilized society because it is the root cause of refinement. It is fear that modifies instincts. Anxiety related to social disapproval is critical in the development of morality. Fear of punishment is the operating force in law-abiding civilian life. Poor fear conditioning has been cited as a predisposing factor to crime. Research has consistently shown that fear-processing systems and fear responses are deficient in individuals with an antisocial personality disorder. Children who demonstrated fearless behavior also revealed less empathy and an inability to identify facial expressions of fear, whereas identification of other emotions was intact. Fear of dangerous consequences is the only operating factor that has the potential to bring the required precision and agility, leading to the safe manipulation of advanced technology. Marcus and MacKuen propose that anxiety need not necessarily impact decisions about political rights detrimentally and hence can enhance rather than diminish democratic life.[72]

Chapter Nine

Optimal Anxiety

Anxiety is adaptive only when its benefits exceed its cost. The cost of anxiety includes its unpleasant nature, its impact on physical and psychological health, and the cost of responding to false alarms. Excess anxiety with distress or impairment is morbid and can be devastating. Some instances imply deadly consequences of extreme anxiety, such as drowning and death from snakebites. Humans can float in water if calm enough, but intense anxiety can cause more movements, unsettling buoyancy, and thus drowning. Anxiety causes increased heart rate and rapid spread of venom after a snakebite. Extreme anxiety may potentially cause cardiac arrest.

Finding optimal anxiety is difficult. Anxiety is a function of anticipation of danger; anxiety is irrelevant once an untoward incident has occurred. Loewenstein et al. make a critical distinction in this context.[1] They divide emotions into anticipatory and anticipated ones. Anticipatory emotions are experienced at the time when a decision is made and the outcome of the decision is anticipated. Anxiety experienced during consenting to a surgical procedure with anticipation of a dreaded outcome is an example of anticipatory emotion.

On the other hand, anticipated emotions are primarily related to experiencing expected outcomes in the future. In other words, they are the consequences of the outcome rather than anticipation itself. In the above example, guilt upon experiencing a complication of surgery—an anticipated outcome—is an anticipated emotion.

OPTIMAL ANXIETY: QUANTITATIVE AND PROBABILISTIC VIEWS

Anxiety is related to the probability of danger rather than its certainty. Also, as we saw in chapter 4, anxiety is decided by the estimated cost of a dangerous outcome.[2] If the outcome has the potential for serious injuries, it may cause more anxiety than the outcome that signifies the possible loss of a small amount of money. The survival or safety benefit of anxiety is determined by the probability of danger and its cost. These benefits of anxiety are thus probabilistically defined. The adaptive function of anxiety depends on the estimates of future danger as accurately as possible. The risk estimate has a subjective element—people who read news about crimes and accidents may overestimate the risk.[3] Every decision is made in the shadow of uncertainty and future risk.

In defining optimal anxiety, the occurrence of false alarms must be considered along with the cost of missing actual danger. The ratio of the cost of anxiety response to a false threat (unnecessary anxiety) to the cost of missing real danger is one component in determining optimal anxiety. The other factor is the ratio of the probability of danger happening to the probability of danger not happening. Therefore, the threshold for and the range of optimal anxiety response is a mathematical concept.

The cost an individual pays for missing a danger gives the degree of vulnerability. The threshold for anxiety reaction goes down when the individual's vulnerability and probability of danger are high and the cost of a false alarm is low. When all other factors are equal, the cost of anxiety is increased heart rate, vigilance, and unpleasant sensation, but the cost of missing a danger could be paying with one's life. In the modern world, many industries are unwilling to take any chances because of concerns about human safety. For instance, fire-extinguishing services activate their responses and arrive at the target quickly. The occurrence of false alarms, which is often the case, does not eliminate this practice. Fire poses a life-threatening danger. The cost of not responding to an actual fire far exceeds the cost of responding to a false alarm. Anxiety is the root factor behind such a low-risk threshold to activate safety measures and zero-error tolerance. When the ratio of the cost of responding to a false alarm to the cost of not responding to a genuine danger is at its lowest, the threshold for errors is kept at zero. Penney et al. propose that selection pressure has favored a response to false alarms over a lack of response to real dangerous alarms, leading to the preservation of anxiety across species.[4]

Marks and Nesse make insightful remarks in the above context.[5] Humans are preconditioned to respond to crude, primitive stimuli that originally induced florid fear reactions. This category includes height, animals, and other stimuli, such as loud noise. The threats in the modern world are different, as seen in the previous chapters, and they elicit either little or inadequate anxiety. Trivial stimuli such as noise can cause fear, which may not serve any purpose. At the same time, mild chest discomfort may not cause significant anxiety, while it could be a sign of an underlying heart attack. Therefore, there is a disconnection between the dangerous nature of anxiety-provoking situations and the degree and functions of the anxiety response. Anxiety may irrelevantly occur to primitive but otherwise safe stimuli such as standing on a tall bridge, flight travel, an animal safely cared for in a zoo, or fireworks. This is a biased reaction as they occur because of the preconditioned brain requiring little experience with these stimuli, which, at the same time, are otherwise largely innocuous. The cost of anxiety in these situations is a false alarm, unnecessary preparedness, along with costly biological reactions such as massive adrenaline surge. Misreading these stimuli also occurs at the expense of diversion from harmful threats in the modern era—dangerous effects of smoking, other substance abuse, infectious diseases, dependence on online games and social media, weapons, wars, and industrial accidents. More people die from guns than snakes, but attentional salience goes to snakes. Modern threats are incapable of eliciting robust anxiety responses as original crude stimuli do and are sometimes accepted with tranquility. This kind of fracture between the nature of stimuli and the adaptive purpose of anxious response undermines the problem of achieving optimal anxiety. Essentially, optimal anxiety refers to the level of anxiety that brings the best task performance. Some authors found that anxiety below the middle split on anxiety-rating-scale scores or a relatively low level of anxiety improved performance.[6]

Hollandsworth et al. observed that enhanced performance among less anxious subjects was associated with a subjective appraisal of anxiety as facilitative. They recommend training highly anxious subjects to relabel their anxiety as facilitative instead of trying to reduce anxiety by relaxation.[7] Nonetheless, it is difficult to draw a quantitative line that divides true debilitative and facilitative anxiety in light of unexpected results. Students with moderate motivation levels also experienced debilitative anxiety (they felt pressure to study), and there was no significant difference in performance between those who experienced debilitative and facilitative anxiety.[8]

Studies have consistently demonstrated that a high level of anxiety adversely impacts test performance.[9] Subjective appraisal of anxiety and its meaning is important in this regard. Stress level can vary depending on what meaning one ascribes to anxiety and the situation, such as the task under question. Stress results from the cognitive evaluation and the subsequent awareness and meaning of the situation. Such evaluative stress is not necessarily the same as anxiety. Stress arises from a demand placed on the mind by an external task or threat; anxiety arises internally and can be present with physiological manifestations without constant awareness. So, people can have a high level of anxiety but a low level of stress and vice versa.

Experts have proposed that attentional shift and stress appraisal could mediate the adverse effects of high anxiety levels.[10] For example, with increased stress, attention in highly anxious individuals is shifted toward internal personalized and self-orientated responses rather than external task performance.[11] The evaluative meaning of stress is perhaps the mediating factor behind poor performance. This is supported by findings obtained by a study that showed improved performance when anxious individuals were given a test under humorous conditions.[12] It was found that humor favorably affected performance, possibly by reducing anxiety in individuals with a high level of anxiety. However, it may be noted that it is not just humor that improved performance because moderately anxious individuals performed at a lower level under humorous conditions compared with highly anxious individuals under humorous conditions. The findings imply that performance efficiency could be a product of the interaction between anxiety and humor. Humor-mediated anxiety reduction would facilitate performance only if anxiety is above the critical level required for performance. This study demonstrated how stress-reducing interventions may help optimize anxiety.

One might anticipate that low anxiety and stress would allow subjects to focus on the task and improve performance. Counterintuitively, this was not the case, according to another report. The performance of the low-anxious and low-stress group was lower than expected and not significantly different from the high-anxiety and high-stress group.[13] The low-anxiety and high-stress groups and the high-anxiety and low-stress groups performed well. These findings are in tune with the Yerkes-Dodson performance curve; increased arousal from stress may facilitate performance in the low-anxious group, and increased anxiety acts as a motivating factor in a low-stress environment.[14] A combination of a high level of anxiety and stress arising from evaluative meaning is deleterious and nonoptimal. Likewise, low-level anxiety and low stress levels are also suboptimal because of a lack of motivation and arousal. In a nutshell, too low anxiety without stress arousal and too high anxiety without stress reduction strategies, such as humor, are detrimental.[15] A high level of anxiety with stress-relieving measures and low anxiety with stress arousal may produce a balanced and optimal performance level.

Optimal Anxiety: Qualitative and Consequentialist Concepts

Anxiety is not the only response in the living world that needs regulation for adaptive functions. The inflammatory response is a classic example. While inflammatory responses are essential for survival, dysregulated inflammation can be lethal when physiological systems confront insults such as an infection. *Anxiety* is the prototype emotion that manifests with both adaptive and maladaptive features. While morbid anxiety and various anxiety disorders are maladaptive, undesirable, and unwelcome, anxiety itself need not be seen as an unwanted human experience. Although optimal anxiety is a theoretical construct, the view of anxiety as an absolutely hateful emotion is untenable. Awareness and acknowledgment of anxiety's beneficial effects can promote a balanced view of anxiety.

Studies on individuals with normal adaptive anxiety are not as many as the studies of morbid anxiety. Such investigations can throw more light into otherwise non-pathological anxiety. Indeed, it is more practical to define morbid anxiety than normal anxiety. There is more than one dimension of normality. According to the statistical norm, anxiety is almost a universal phenomenon. Anxiety as such is never abnormal. This should be emphasized because the term anxiety invites memories of a negative mental state, a state of illness, and abnormal functioning. It is not always the case. Normal anxiety may be difficult to envisage, although it is a universal human condition.

Coming to the functional norm, we have already seen that anxiety serves different functions. In this way, anxiety is normal, adaptive, and present in humans by default. We can study anxiety without necessarily defining normal anxiety. However, we need a more precise concept of what constitutes abnormal or morbid anxiety. We have seen anxiety disorders in detail in chapter 3. Arguably, any level of anxiety below the threshold of an anxiety disorder can be optimal anxiety; only its degree varies.

Optimal anxiety is desirable since it is adaptive, functional, and beneficial. Nevertheless, how do we achieve optimal anxiety? First, the notion that anxiety is always a destructive emotion needs to be dissected and deconstructed. Educational systems need revision and may convey that while excess anxiety is disabling, optimal anxiety is a primary and constantly operating survival mechanism. Moreover, the dangerous consequences of a lack of adequate anxiety must be stressed without qualifications. By several means, if excess anxiety is unpleasant and debilitative, a lack of anxiety can be catastrophic and fatal. The former is certainly distressing, but the latter is destructive. With explanation and education, the concept of optimal anxiety can be developed. Awareness of the need for anxiety itself may facilitate the development of optimal anxiety.

Bravery is regarded as a positive quality, and cowardice is portrayed as a symbol of weakness. Conventional wisdom, however, does not always hold. It depends on the context and the content. For instance, what someone is brave about can be a determinant factor. Bravery for a drive on a busy freeway is not the same as bravery for driving through floodwater. Being a coward in meeting people differs from being a coward while seeing someone with a loaded gun. The purpose that bravery and cowardice serve defines whether it is a positive or negative quality, adaptive or maladaptive. There is no blanket qualification. The outcome of fear and anxiety will determine whether it is optimal or morbid anxiety. When the anxiety of failure motivates a student to learn thoroughly, when the anxiety of deterioration of illness in a patient forces a doctor to consider extraordinary treatments, when the anxiety of contracting an infectious disease prohibits a person's attendance at a gathering, or when fear of punishment deters someone from committing a crime, such anxiety has a likelihood of being optimal even when it comes with an expected cost, the unpleasantness of anxiety.

On the other hand, if anxiety is mild but the amount of anxiety does not result in a beneficial outcome, it is not optimal anxiety. Conversely, the anxiety of failure that leads to avoidance of examination, the anxiety of deterioration of illness that results in impaired attention and erroneous treatment decisions, the anxiety of contracting infection that leads to complete reclusion, and unfounded fear of punishment that leads to self-depreciation and guilt all are maladaptive anxiety and, hence, nonoptimal. In this context, optimal anxiety is defined from a consequentialist perspective; whether anxiety is optimal depends on its consequences.

From the above views, it is argued that the purpose anxiety serves determines whether it is optimal anxiety. This follows that optimal anxiety is not necessarily related to the magnitude of the anxiety. Let us consider a few other scenarios. Highly threatening situations such as fire or a bomb threat cause intense anxiety, followed by avoiding these dangers, whereas avoiding late arrival for daily work may not require intense anxiety. Similarly, if passion is vital for risky behavior like climbing Mount Everest, extreme anxiety will be required to overcome this passion. If the desire is not so strong, only a tiny amount of anxiety may be sufficient to act as a deterrent. Therefore, the degree of anxiety as such does not decide optimal anxiety. This consequentialist view is a departure from the quantitative and mathematical concept of optimal anxiety derived from the ratio of the cost of responding to a false threat divided by not responding to a true danger. We have seen how anxiety was preserved during the evolutionary process because of its survival benefits. This, however, is an incomplete picture. Evolution has come with by-products: cognitive biases and inappropriate anxiety reactions.

Decisions in life pose risks. Risks are evaluated cognitively (e.g., probability of an untoward outcome) and effectively (feeling of dread). Decisions involving risks are end products of the above factors operating in combination and opposition. Equally possible is the influence that cognition and emotion have on each other. Sound and objective appreciation of a situation may conclude a high probability of a dangerous outcome and hence more fear with subsequence avoidance of the dangerous outcome. Modern organizations have developed tools to systematically assess probabilities of dangerous and desired outcomes. Such an organized approach is particularly relevant given the influence of emotions on probabilistic estimates of danger; strong passion may lead to underestimation of the risk, and intense anxiety may lead to overestimation of the risk. As presented earlier, by default, the human brain is wired in such a way that passion defeats reason. While emotions occur with and without cognitive evaluation, the impact of cognitive evaluation on risk appraisal is mediated through emotions. Anxious individuals tend to make risk-aversive decisions. People become anxious as a knee-jerk reaction without examination of facts. They can also become anxious after becoming aware of facts. Facts influence decisions only by generating certain emotions. Otherwise, facts remain as facts without impacting decisions or motivations. Emotions cause approach or avoidant behavior, whereas cognitive evaluation results in true-false distinction.[16] Emotions are instantaneous without involving cognitive processes except for the essential awareness of the stimulus.[17] Noise, for example, can produce fear even when we do not know the source of the noise. Emotions are rapid and automatic reactions.

In a vivid account, Weinstein illustrates the impact of extraordinary personal trauma on victims' future behavior and lives. He discussed four areas of trauma: automobile accidents, criminal victimization other than rape, natural disasters, and myocardial infarction. Although beneficial in certain aspects, as discussed in a previous chapter, fear appeals may deter healthy choices. For instance, in one study, fear-inducing communication led to behavioral changes in smoking, but participants refused to get X-rays because of fear of detecting a serious disease.[18] Such anxiety may cause harm by inducing defensive behavior and avoiding active interventions. Although it is anxiety that is the operative force, it is not adaptive.

Optimal anxiety, therefore, requires future discussions and balanced consideration of the detrimental effects of anxiety as well as its adaptive and beneficial effects. Intensity, duration, context, and purpose of anxiety, as incidental factors such as evaluative stress, may give an understanding of optimal anxiety. Extreme maladaptive emotions, anxiety in particular, are not optimal and unwelcome. The amount of anxiety sufficient to avert danger is difficult to define. As a rule of thumb, anxiety sufficient to motivate one to take caution in risky situations, avoid potentially dangerous exposures, seek conformity to societal norms, and maintain safe behaviors is optimal anxiety. Also, anxiety sufficient to motivate action without impairing performance is optimal. As a stark reality, the balance hangs on a thin line, and one might wonder if this is a theoretical construct rather than a practice in real life. Still, the concept of optimal anxiety is critical for a comprehensive discussion about anxiety.

Chapter Ten

Conclusions

Fear has many eyes and can see underground.
—Miguel de Cervantes[1]

Unmistakably, anxiety is felt and viewed as a negative emotion. As described in the previous chapters, its unpleasantness is, however, its advantage and a signature of the survival of living creatures—the aretaic and evaluative aspects of anxiety make it a unique phenomenon in this regard. Morals and manners change, but anxiety remains over ages. Anxiety predated humans: it was described in antiquity; it characterized the middle age ("the age of anxiety" with a morbid "psyche" with a sense of impending doom) precisely as it does in the present time (the modern era of anxiety). The world is an uncertain place, and human life hangs on coincidences. Anxiety is, therefore, a rule in the biological world. It is a messenger, a representative of the imperfect architecture of the universe. It is perhaps the only emotion with features of both a negative quality and survival value. Anxiety disciplines thoughts and controls behavior. It is the motivator for our actions. In a way, it is a beautiful phenomenon in that humans learn that life is based not only on positive emotions, such as love and happiness, but also on negative emotions; anxiety is prototypal of the negative emotions, which must be embraced for welfare and survival.

The above account is limited by difficulties in deriving empirical findings in social psychology and their interpretation. An in-depth analysis of the studies quoted above was not performed. It is acknowledged that the arguments presented above could be biased. The studies discussed above were based on participants' subjective reports, which could not be objectively measured. Subjective reports may have considerable variability. Therefore, there is an inherent limitation in the generalizability of such findings. Moreover, the validity of some of these studies is questionable because they included small sample sizes, the methodology was not rigorous, and the findings were not reproduced.

An unexplored philosophical territory of anxiety is the ultimate powerlessness of man. Anxiety is a product of imagination. On the other hand, if imagination comes with positive content, it would have served as the last solace for suffering. On the contrary, when imagination involves threat, it preempts all positive emotions. Anxiety thus becomes the dead end; it is irreducible in its origin and represents the final destiny.

Given that anxiety is fundamentally a normal and adaptive phenomenon, pathologizing anxiety requires a careful and sophisticated approach. Societal views, cultures, art, and folklore depict anxiety as a character weakness or morbidity that needs professional help from psychiatric services. Medicalization of anxiety carries a risk of losing the forest for the trees. At times, the challenge in psychiatry is not in treating morbid anxiety but in confidently asserting that non-pathological anxiety is an inseparable part of human existence and does not need further psychiatric evaluation or treatment. Differentiating pathological anxiety, an anxiety disorder, from normal and functional anxiety is at the heart of psychiatric practice. The province of psychiatry is more than diagnostic classifications or criteria. There are several effective medications and psychological strategies to control morbid anxiety, but the development of a holistic view of the human predicament is beyond the diagnostic formulation of an individual patient; it very much requires deep roots in social psychology and philosophy. Indeed, group psychology evolved before individual psychopathology. Anxiety becomes a complete concept when placed in a societal context. This was particularly evident during the COVID-19 pandemic when a lack of adequate anxiety and denial of the possibility of the infection and its severity and mortality were associated with ravaging waves and peaks of infections worldwide. Similarly, psychiatry should incorporate a view of anxiety embedded in philosophy.

Conclusions

As long as the human brain functions with strong influence from the limbic cortex and its elaborations in the frontal cortex, anxiety reactions will continue with their unique features in adaptive and morbid forms. For the time when bad is stronger than good, and man is more motivated to avoid bad than pursue good, anxiety will remain.

The enemy of anxiety and, hence, life is the denial of realities. While moderate denial is necessary to preserve mental equilibrium and avoid mental collapse, this defense mechanism may also lead to decisions incompatible with survival. Defense mechanisms are like immunity and inflammation. Immature defense mechanisms may go wrong when they are unregulated. They thus become nasty and threaten life, bringing devastating consequences. Denial appears to be the most dangerous because it eliminates anxiety. The mind then becomes a dangerous organ.

Notes

Chapter 1: Introduction

1. Marks If, Nesse RM. Fear and fitness: An evolutionary analysis of anxiety disorders. *Ethology and Sociobiology.* 1994;15(5):247–61.
2. Crocq MA. A history of anxiety: from Hippocrates to DSM. *Dialogues Clin Neurosci.* 2015;17(3):319–25.
3. Solomon RC. *The Passions: Emotions and the Meaning of Life.* New York: Hackett Publishing Company; 1993.
4. Watts CG, Drummond M, Goumas C, et al. Sunscreen use and melanoma risk among young Australian adults. *JAMA Dermatol.* 2018;154(9):1001–9.
5. Tannenbaum MB, Hepler J, Zimmerman RS, et al. Appealing to fear: A meta-analysis of fear appeal effectiveness and theories. *Psychol Bull.* 2015;141(6):1178–204.
6. Coplan J, Hodulik S, Mathew S, et al. The Relationship between Intelligence and Anxiety: An Association with Subcortical White Matter Metabolism. *Frontiers in Evolutionary Neuroscience.* 2012;3.
7. Waters TR, Dick RB. Evidence of health risks associated with prolonged standing at work and intervention effectiveness. *Rehabil Nurs.* 2015;40(3):148–65.
8. Crocq. A history of anxiety; Jackson P, Everts J. Anxiety as Social Practice. *Environment and Planning A: Economy and Space.* 2010;42(11):2791–806.
9. Pizarro Obaid F. Sigmund Freud and Otto Rank: debates and confrontations about anxiety and birth. *Int J Psychoanal.* 2012;93(3):693–715; Rank O. (1929). *The Trauma of Birth.* London: Kegan Paul Trench Trubner & Co Limited. Reprinted by Routledge, in 1999.
10. Panksepp J, Fuchs T, Iacobucci P. The basic neuroscience of emotional experiences in mammals: The case of subcortical FEAR circuitry and implications for clinical anxiety. *Applied Animal Behaviour Science.* 2011;129(1):1–17.
11. Perusini JN, Fanselow MS. Neurobehavioral perspectives on the distinction between fear and anxiety. *Learn Mem.* 2015;22(9):417–25.
12. Kurth C. Moral Anxiety and Moral Agency. *Oxford Studies in Normative Ethics.* 2015;5:171–95.
13. Walker DL, Toufexis DJ, Davis M. Role of the bed nucleus of the stria terminalis versus the amygdala in fear, stress, and anxiety. *Eur J Pharmacol.* 2003;463(1–3):199–216.

14. Steckler T. The neuropsychology of stress. In: Steckler T, Kalin NH, Reul JMHM, eds. *Handbook of Stress and the Brain Part 1: The Neurobiology of Stress*. Amsterdam: Elsevier; 2005, 25.

15. Koolhaas JM, Bartolomucci A, Buwalda B, et al. Stress revisited: a critical evaluation of the stress concept. *Neurosci Biobehav Rev.* 2011;35(5):1291–301.

16. Tateo L. Giambattista Vico and the new psychological science. 2017.

17. Svendsen L. *A Philosophy of Fear*. London: Reaktion Books; 2008.

18. Katschnig H, Nutzinger DO, Nouzak A, Schanda H, David H. [Depression and anxiety—a study for validating subtypes of depression]. *Psychiatr Prax.* 1990;17(4):136–43.

19. Crocq M-A. The history of generalized anxiety disorder as a diagnostic category. *Dialogues Clin Neurosci.* 2017;19(2):107–16.

20. Berrios GE. Anxiety and cognate disorders. *The History of Mental Symptoms: Descriptive psychopathology since the nineteenth century*. 1996.

21. Blanchard DC, Hynd AL, Minke KA, Minemoto T, Blanchard RJ. Human defensive behaviors to threat scenarios show parallels to fear- and anxiety-related defense patterns of non-human mammals. *Neurosci Biobehav Rev.* 2001;25(7–8):761–70.

22. Martin P. The epidemiology of anxiety disorders: a review. *Dialogues Clin Neurosci.* 2003;5(3):281–98.

23. Gilbert P, McEwan K, Catarino F, Baião R, Palmeira L. Fears of happiness and compassion in relationship with depression, alexithymia, and attachment security in a depressed sample. *British Journal of Clinical Psychology*. 2014;53(2):228–44.

24. Rakic P. Evolution of the neocortex: a perspective from developmental biology. *Nature Reviews Neuroscience.* 2009;10(10):724–35.

25. York GK, Steinberg DA. Hughlings Jackson's theory of recovery. *Neurology.* 1995;45(4):834–38; Ribot T. *Diseases of memory: an essay in the positive psychology*. New York: D. Appleton and Company; 1882.

26. LeDoux JE. *The emotional brain: The mysterious underpinnings of emotional life*. New York: Simon & Schuster; 1996.

27. Frijda NH. *The laws of emotion*. Mahwah, NJ: Lawrence Erlbaum Associates Publishers; 2007.

28. Clark A. *Hack Your Anxiety: How to Make Anxiety Work for You in Life, Love, and All That You Do*. New York: Sourcebooks; 2018.

29. Barlow DH. *Anxiety and Its Disorders: The Nature and Treatment of Anxiety and Panic (2nd ed.)*. New York: The Guilford Press; 2002.

30. Coplan, et al. The relationship between intelligence and anxiety.

31. Selye H. Stress without distress. In: Serban G, ed. *Psychopathology of Human Adaptation*. Boston, MA: Springer US; 1976:137–46.

Chapter 2: The Origin and Development of Fear

1. Barlow. *Anxiety and Its Disorders*.

2. Macnab RM, Koshland DE, Jr. The gradient-sensing mechanism in bacterial chemotaxis. *Proc Natl Acad Sci U S A.* 1972;69(9):2509–12.

Notes

3. Ibid.; Fanselow MS. Associative vs topographical accounts of the immediate shock-freezing deficit in rats: Implications for the response selection rules governing species-specific defensive reactions. *Learning and Motivation*. 1986;17(1):16–39.

4. Marlin NA. Contextual associations in trace conditioning. *Animal Learning & Behavior*. 1981;9(4):519–23.

5. Marks, Nesse. Fear and fitness.

6. Marks IM. *Fears and phobias*. London: Heinemann; 1969.

7. Poulton R, Menzies RG. Fears born and bred: Toward a more inclusive theory of fear acquisition. *Behaviour Research and Therapy*. 2002;40(2):197–208.

8. Hoehl S, Hellmer K, Johansson M, Gredebäck G. Itsy bitsy spider...: Infants react with increased arousal to spiders and snakes. *Frontiers in Psychology*. 2017;8.

9. Poulton R, Davies S, Menzies RG, Langley JD, Silva PA. Evidence for a non-associative model of the acquisition of a fear of heights. *Behav Res Ther*. 1998;36(5):537–44.

10. Gibson EJ, Walk RD. The "visual cliff." *Scientific American*. 1960;202(4):64–71.

11. Adolph KE, Kretch KS, LoBue V. Fear of heights in infants? *Curr Dir Psychol Sci*. 2014;23(1):60–66.

12. Gibson EJ, Walk RD. The "visual cliff."

13. Scarr S, Salapatek P. Patterns of fear development during infancy. *Merrill-Palmer Quarterly*. 1970;16(1):53–90.

14. Ibid.

15. Hebb DO. On the nature of fear. *Psychological review*. 1946;53 5:259–76.

16. Ibid.

17. Valentine CW. The innate bases of fear. *The Journal of Genetic Psychology*. 1991;152(4):501–27.

18. Hebb. On the nature of fear.

19. Jones MC. Emotional development. In Murchison C, ed. *A handbook of child psychology, 2nd ed.* Worcester, MA: Clark University Press; 1933.

20. Jersild AT, Holmes FB. Some factors in the development of children's fears. *The Journal of Experimental Education*. 1935;4(2):133–41.

21. Ibid.; Bauer DH. An exploratory study of developmental changes in children's fears. *J Child Psychol Psychiatry*. 1976;17(1):69–74.; Hall GS. A study of fears. *The American Journal of Psychology*. 1897;8(2):147–249; Angelino H, Shedd CL. Shifts in the content of fears and worries relative to chronological age. *Proceedings of the Oklahoma Academy of Science*. 1953;34:180–86.

22. Burnham JJ, Gullone E. The fear survey schedule for children—II: A psychometric investigation with American data. *Behav Res Ther*. 1997;35(2):165–73.

23. Slaughter V, Griffiths M. Death understanding and fear of death in young children. *Clinical Child Psychology and Psychiatry*. 2007;12(4):525–35.

24. Poulton R, Trainor P, Stanton W, McGee R, Davies S, Silva P. The (in)stability of adolescent fears. *Behav Res Ther*. 1997;35(2):159–63.

25. Spence SH, McCathie H. The stability of fears in children: A two-year prospective study: a research note. *J Child Psychol Psychiatry*. 1993 May;34(4):579–827

26. Hall, G. S. A study of fears. *The American Journal of Psychology*. 1897; 8(2):147–249.

27. Grillon C, Baas JM, Pine DS, et al. The benzodiazepine alprazolam dissociates contextual fear from cued fear in humans as assessed by fear-potentiated startle. *Biol Psychiatry*. 2006;60(7):760–66.

28. Wolpe J, Rachman S. Psychoanalytic evidence: A critique based on Freud's case of Little Hans. *Journal of Nervous and Mental Disease*. 1960;131:1355145.

29. Grillon et al. The benzodiazepine alprazolam dissociates.

30. Grupe DW, Nitschke JB. Uncertainty and anticipation in anxiety: an integrated neurobiological and psychological perspective. *Nature Reviews Neuroscience*. 2013;14(7): 488–501.

31. Ibid.

32. Mowrer OH. Two-factor learning theory: Summary and comment. *Psychological Review*. 1951;58(5):350–54.

33. Mowrer OH. A stimulus-response analysis of anxiety and its role as a reinforcing agent. *Psychological Review*. 1939;46(6):553–65.

34. Rachman S. The conditioning theory of fear acquisition: A critical examination. *Behaviour Research and Therapy*. 1977;15:375–87.

35. Bandura A. *Social Learning Theory*. Morristown, NJ: General Learning Press; 1971.

36. Askew C, Field AP. The vicarious learning pathway to fear 40 years on. *Clin Psychol Rev*. 2008;28(7):1249–65.

37. Gerull F, Rapee RM. Mother knows best: Effects of maternal modelling on the acquisition of fear and avoidance behaviour in toddlers. *Behaviour research and therapy*. 2002;40 3:279–87; Olsson A, Phelps EA. Social learning of fear. *Nat Neurosci*. 2007;10(9):1095–102; Field AP, Argyris NG, Knowles KA. Who's afraid of the big bad wolf: A prospective paradigm to test Rachman's indirect pathways in children. *Behav Res Ther*. 2001;39(11):1259–76.

38. Gerull, Rapee. Mother knows best.

39. Hugdahl K, Öhman A. Effects of instruction on acquisition and extinction of electrodermal responses to fear-relevant stimuli. *Journal of Experimental Psychology: Human Learning and Memory*. 1977;3(5):608–18.

40. Field, Argyris, Knowles. Who's afraid of the big bad wolf.

41. Lebowitz ER, Shic F, Campbell D, MacLeod J, Silverman WK. Avoidance moderates the association between mothers' and children's fears: findings from a novel motion-tracking behavioral assessment. *Depress Anxiety*. 2015;32(2):91–98.

42. Olsson, Phelps. Social learning of fear.

43. Golkar A, Olsson A. Immunization against social fear learning. *Journal of Experimental Psychology: General*. 2016;145(6):665–71.

44. Gunnar MR, Hostinar CE, Sanchez MM, Tottenham N, Sullivan RM. Parental buffering of fear and stress neurobiology: Reviewing parallels across rodent, monkey, and human models. *Soc Neurosci*. 2015;10(5):474–78.

45. Eley TC, McAdams TA, Rijsdijk FV, et al. The intergenerational transmission of anxiety: A children-of-twins study. *Am J Psychiatry*. 2015;172(7):630–37.

46. Hekmat H. Origins and development of human fear reactions. *Journal of Anxiety Disorders*. 1987;1(3):197–218.

47. Ekman P. Emotions inside out. 130 Years after Darwin's "The Expression of the Emotions in Man and Animal." *Ann N Y Acad Sci.* 2003;1000:1–6.
48. Marks, Nesse. Fear and fitness.
49. Darwin C. *The Expression of the Emotions In Man And Animals: With an Introduction, Afterword and Commentaries by.* Oxford University Press; 2009; LeDoux JE. Evolution of human emotion: A view through fear. *Prog Brain Res.* 2012;195:431–42.
50. Ekman. Emotions inside out.
51. Ibid.
52. Dodd MS, Papineau D, Grenne T, et al. Evidence for early life in Earth's oldest hydrothermal vent precipitates. *Nature.* 2017;543(7643):60–64; Cavalazzi B, Lemelle L, Simionovici A, et al. Cellular remains in a ~3.42-billion-year-old subseafloor hydrothermal environment. *Science Advances.* 2021;7(29):eabf3963.
53. Marks, Nesse. Fear and fitness.
54. Coplan et al. The relationship between intelligence and anxiety.
55. Ibid.
56. Ibid.
57. Kendler KS, Gardner CO, Annas P, Neale MC, Eaves LJ, Lichtenstein P. A longitudinal twin study of fears from middle childhood to early adulthood: Evidence for a developmentally dynamic genome. *Arch Gen Psychiatry.* 2008;65(4):421–29.
58. Van Houtem CM, Laine ML, Boomsma DI, Ligthart L, van Wijk AJ, De Jongh A. A review and meta-analysis of the heritability of specific phobia subtypes and corresponding fears. *J Anxiety Disord.* 2013;27(4):379–88.
59. Torgersen S. Genetic factors in anxiety disorders. *Arch Gen Psychiatry.* 1983;40(10):1085–89.
60. Freedman D. Hereditary control of early social behaviour. In Foss, B, ed. *Determinants of infant behavior III.* New York: Wiley; 1965.
61. Shields J. Twins brought up apart. *Eugen Rev.* 1958;50(2):115–23.
62. Distel MA, Vink JM, Willemsen G, Middeldorp CM, Merckelbach HLGJ, Boomsma DI. Heritability of self-reported phobic fear. *Behav Genet.* 2008;38(1):24–33; Kendler KS, Neale MC, Kessler RC, Heath AC, Eaves LJ. The genetic epidemiology of phobias in women: The interrelationship of agoraphobia, social phobia, situational phobia, and simple phobia. *Archives of General Psychiatry.* 1992;49(4):273–81.
63. Villafuerte S, Burmeister M. Untangling genetic networks of panic, phobia, fear and anxiety. *Genome Biology.* 2003;4(8):224.
64. Freud S. (1926). Inhibitions, symptoms, and anxiety. In *The Standard edition of the complete psychological works of Sigmund Freud.* London: Hogarth Press; 1975.
65. Sullivan HS. *The interpersonal theory of psychiatry.* New York: W W Norton & Co; 1953.
66. Bowlby J. *Attachment and loss. Volume II.* 1973.
67. Feeney B, Collins N. Predictors of caregiving in adult Intimate relationships: An attachment theoretical perspective. *Journal of personality and social psychology.* 2001;80:972–94.

68. Kerns KA, Brumariu LE. Is Insecure Parent-Child Attachment a Risk Factor for the Development of Anxiety in Childhood or Adolescence? *Child Dev Perspect.* 2014;8(1):12–17.

69. Simpson J, Kim J, Fillo J, et al. Attachment and the management of empathic accuracy in relationship-threatening situations. *Personality & Social Psychology Bulletin.* 2011;37:242–54.

70. Hassabis D, Kumaran D, Vann SD, Maguire EA. Patients with hippocampal amnesia cannot imagine new experiences. *Proceedings of the National Academy of Sciences.* 2007;104(5):1726–31.

71. Adolphs R, Tranel D, Hamann S, et al. Recognition of facial emotion in nine individuals with bilateral amygdala damage. *Neuropsychologia.* 1999;37(10):1111–17; Bechara A, Damasio H, Tranel D, Damasio AR. Deciding advantageously before knowing the advantageous strategy. *Science.* 1997;275(5304):1293–95.

72. Rachman. The conditioning theory of fear acquisition.

73. Hekmat. Origins and development of human fear reactions.

74. Blake DD, Keane TM, Wine PR, Mora C, Taylor KL, Lyons JA. Prevalence of PTSD symptoms in combat veterans seeking medical treatment. *Journal of Traumatic Stress.* 1990;3(1):15–27; Breslau N, Davis GC, Andreski P, Peterson E. Traumatic events and posttraumatic stress disorder in an urban population of young adults. *Arch Gen Psychiatry.* 1991;48(3):216–22.

CHAPTER 3: UNFRIENDLY ANXIETY

1. Borkovec TD, Robinson E, Pruzinsky T, DePree JA. Preliminary exploration of worry: Some characteristics and processes. *Behaviour Research and Therapy.* 1983;21(1):9–16; Borkovec TD, Inz J. The nature of worry in generalized anxiety disorder: a predominance of thought activity. *Behav Res Ther.* 1990;28(2):153–58.

2. Rosen JB, Schulkin J. From normal fear to pathological anxiety. *Psychological Review.* 1998;105(2):325–50.

3. Coles ME, Turk CL, Heimberg RG. Memory bias for threat in generalized anxiety disorder: the potential importance of stimulus relevance. *Cogn Behav Ther.* 2007;36(2):65–73; Coles ME, Heimberg RG. Memory biases in the anxiety disorders: Current status. *Clin Psychol Rev.* 2002;22(4):587–627.

4. Kessler RC, Berglund P, Demler O, Jin R, Merikangas KR, Walters EE. Lifetime prevalence and age-of-onset distributions of DSM-IV disorders in the National Comorbidity Survey Replication. *Arch Gen Psychiatry.* 2005;62(6):593–602.

5. Canuto A, Weber K, Baertschi M, et al. Anxiety disorders in old age: Psychiatric comorbidities, quality of life, and prevalence according to age, gender, and country. *Am J Geriatr Psychiatry.* 2018;26(2):174–85; Welzel FD, Stein J, Röhr S, et al. Prevalence of anxiety symptoms and their association with loss experience in a large cohort sample of the oldest-old. Results of the AgeCoDe/AgeQualiDe study. *Front Psychiatry.* 2019;10:285.

6. Roest Annelieke M, Martens Elisabeth J, de Jonge P, Denollet J. Anxiety and risk of incident coronary heart disease. *Journal of the American College of Cardiology.* 2010;56(1):38–46.

NOTES

7. Liukkonen T, Räsänen P, Jokelainen J, et al. The association between anxiety and C-reactive protein (CRP) levels: Results from the Northern Finland 1966 Birth Cohort Study. *European Psychiatry.* 2011;26(6):363–69.

8. Mendlowicz MV, Stein MB. Quality of life in individuals with anxiety disorders. *Am J Psychiatry.* 2000;157(5):669–82; Olatunji BO, Cisler JM, Tolin DF. Quality of life in the anxiety disorders: a meta-analytic review. *Clin Psychol Rev.* 2007;27(5):572–81.

9. Konnopka A, König H. Economic Burden of anxiety disorders: A systematic review and meta-analysis. *Pharmacoeconomics.* 2020;38(1):25–37.

10. Erickson SR, Guthrie S, Vanetten-Lee M, et al. Severity of anxiety and work-related outcomes of patients with anxiety disorders. *Depress Anxiety.* 2009;26(12):1165–71; Waghorn G, Chant D, White P, Whiteford H. Disability, employment and work performance among people with ICD-10 anxiety disorders. *Aust N Z J Psychiatry.* 2005;39(1–2):55–66.

11. Copeland WE, Angold A, Shanahan L, Costello EJ. Longitudinal patterns of anxiety from childhood to adulthood: The Great Smoky Mountains Study. *J Am Acad Child Adolesc Psychiatry.* 2014;53(1):21–33.

12. Woodward LJ, Fergusson DM. Life course outcomes of young people with anxiety disorders in adolescence. *J Am Acad Child Adolesc Psychiatry.* 2001;40(9):1086–93.

13. Reavley NJ, Jorm AF. Stigmatizing attitudes towards people with mental disorders: findings from an Australian National Survey of Mental Health Literacy and Stigma. *Aust N Z J Psychiatry.* 2011;45(12):1086–93.

14. Pittig A, Brand M, Pawlikowski M, Alpers GW. The cost of fear: Avoidant decision making in a spider gambling task. *Journal of Anxiety Disorders.* 2014;28(3):326–34.

15. Craske MG, Rauch SL, Ursano R, Prenoveau J, Pine DS, Zinbarg RE. What is an anxiety disorder? *FOCUS.* 2011;9(3):369–88.

16. Yip JA, Côté S. The emotionally intelligent decision maker: emotion-understanding ability reduces the effect of incidental anxiety on risk taking. *Psychol Sci.* 2013;24(1):48–55.

17. Feeney, Collins. Predictors of caregiving in adult intimate relationships.

18. Zaider TI, Heimberg RG, Iida M. Anxiety disorders and intimate relationships: a study of daily processes in couples. *J Abnorm Psychol.* 2010;119(1):163–73.

CHAPTER 4: NEUROBIOLOGY OF FEAR

1. LeDoux. *The emotional brain*; LeDoux JE, Pine DS. Using neuroscience to help understand fear and anxiety: A two-system framework. *Am J Psychiatry.* 2016;173(11): 1083–93.

2. Johnson DJ. Noradrenergic control of cognition: Global attenuation and an interrupt function. *Med Hypotheses.* 2003;60(5):689–92.

3. Straube T, Mentzel HJ, Miltner WH. Waiting for spiders: brain activation during anticipatory anxiety in spider phobics. *Neuroimage.* 2007;37(4):1427–36.

4. Mobbs D, Yu R, Rowe JB, Eich H, FeldmanHall O, Dalgleish T. Neural activity associated with monitoring the oscillating threat value of a tarantula. *Proceedings of the National Academy of Sciences of the United States of America.* 2010;107(47):20582–86.

5. Alvarez RP, Chen G, Bodurka J, Kaplan R, Grillon C. Phasic and sustained fear in humans elicits distinct patterns of brain activity. *Neuroimage*. 2011;55(1):389–400.

6. Somerville LH, Whalen PJ, Kelley WM. Human bed nucleus of the stria terminalis indexes hypervigilant threat monitoring. *Biol Psychiatry*. 2010;68(5):416–24.

7. Grillon et al. The benzodiazepine alprazolam; Grillon C, Chavis C, Covington MF, Pine DS. Two-week treatment with the selective serotonin reuptake inhibitor citalopram reduces contextual anxiety but not cued fear in healthy volunteers: a fear-potentiated startle study. *Neuropsychopharmacology*. 2009;34(4):964–71.

8. Baldwin DS, Anderson IM, Nutt DJ, et al. Evidence-based guidelines for the pharmacological treatment of anxiety disorders: recommendations from the British Association for Psychopharmacology. *J Psychopharmacol*. 2005;19(6):567–96.

9. Gray TS. Amygdaloid CRF pathways. Role in autonomic, neuroendocrine, and behavioral responses to stress. *Ann N Y Acad Sci*. 1993;697:53–60.

10. Whelan RF, Young IM. The effect of adrenaline and noradrenaline infusions on respiration in man. *Br J Pharmacol Chemother*. 1953;8(1):98–102.

11. Grillon et al. The benzodiazepine alprazolam; Grillon et al. Two-week treatment.

12. Baldwin et al. Evidence-based guidelines for the pharmacological treatment of anxiety disorders.

13. Luu P, Tucker DM, Derryberry D. Anxiety and the motivational basis of working memory. *Cognitive Therapy and Research*. 1998;22(6):577–94.

14. Vuilleumier P, Armony JL, Clarke K, Husain M, Driver J, Dolan RJ. Neural response to emotional faces with and without awareness: event-related fMRI in a parietal patient with visual extinction and spatial neglect. *Neuropsychologia*. 2002;40(12):2156–66.

Chapter 5: Psychological Theories and Philosophy of Fear

1. Butler G, Mathews A. Cognitive processes in anxiety. *Advances in Behaviour Research and Therapy*. 1983;5(1):51–62; Stöber J. Trait anxiety and pessimistic appraisal of risk and chance. *Personality and Individual Differences*. 1997;22(4):465–76.

2. Mitte K. Anxiety and risky decision-making: The role of subjective probability and subjective costs of negative events. *Personality and Individual Differences*. 2007;43(2):243–53; Foa EB, Franklin ME, Perry KJ, Herbert JD. Cognitive biases in generalized social phobia. *Journal of Abnormal Psychology*. 1996;105(3):433–39.

3. Ibid.

4. Barlow DH. Unraveling the mysteries of anxiety and its disorders from the perspective of emotion theory. *American Psychologist*. 2000;55(11):1247–63.

5. Smith A, Ebert E, Broman-Fulks J. The relationship between anxiety and risk taking is moderated by ambiguity. *Personality and Individual Differences*. 2016;95:40–44.

6. Ibid.

7. Shepperd JA, Grace J, Cole LJ, Klein C. Anxiety and Outcome Predictions. *Personality and Social Psychology Bulletin*. 2005;31(2):267–75.

8. Kurth. *Moral Anxiety and Moral Agency*; Vazard J. Epistemic anxiety, adaptive cognition, and obsessive-compulsive disorder. In: *Philosophical Perspectives on Affective Experience and Psychopathology*. 2018:137–58.

9. Han PKJ, Klein WMP, Arora NK. Varieties of uncertainty in health care: a conceptual taxonomy. *Med Decis Making.* 2011;31(6):828–38.
10. Ibid.
11. Mishel MH. Uncertainty in illness. *Image J Nurs Sch.* 1988;20(4):225–32.
12. Vazard. Epistemic anxiety.
13. Barlow. *Anxiety and Its Disorders*; Mineka S, Zinbarg R. Conditioning and ethological models of anxiety disorders: Stress-in-dynamic-context anxiety models. In: *Nebraska Symposium on Motivation, 1995: Perspectives on anxiety, panic, and fear.* Lincoln, NE: University of Nebraska Press; 1996:135–210.
14. Miceli M, Castelfranchi C. Anxiety as an "epistemic" emotion: An uncertainty theory of anxiety. *Anxiety Stress and Coping.* 2005;18:291–319.
15. Sanderson WC, Rapee RM, Barlow DH. The influence of an illusion of control on panic attacks induced via inhalation of 5.5% carbon dioxide-enriched air. *Arch Gen Psychiatry.* 1989;46(2):157–62.
16. Eysenck MW. *Anxiety and cognition: A unified theory.* Hove, England: Psychology Press/Erlbaum (UK) Taylor & Francis; 1997; Williams JMG, Watts FN, MacLeod C, Mathews A. *Cognitive psychology and emotional disorders.* Oxford, England: John Wiley & Sons; 1988.
17. Grupe, Nitschke. Uncertainty and anticipation in anxiety.
18. Marks, Nesse. Fear and fitness.
19. Tomkins SS. *Affect imagery consciousness: The complete edition.* 2008.
20. Izard CE. Basic emotions, natural kinds, emotion schemas, and a new paradigm. *Perspectives on Psychological Science.* 2007;2(3):260–80; Ekman P. An argument for basic emotions. *Cognition and Emotion.* 1992;6(3–4):169–200.
21. Tomkins. Affect imagery consciousness.
22. LeDoux, J. *Anxious: Using the Brain to Understand and Treat Fear and Anxiety.* New York: Penguin Books, 2016.
23. Todd RM, Ehlers MR, Müller DJ, et al. Neurogenetic variations in norepinephrine availability enhance perceptual vividness. *The Journal of Neuroscience.* 2015;35(16):6506–16.
24. Bevilacqua L, Goldman D. Genetics of emotion. *Trends Cogn Sci.* 2011;15(9):401–8.
25. Kierkegaard S. *The concept of anxiety: A simple psychologically orienting deliberation on the dogmatic issue of hereditary sin.* Princeton, NJ: Princeton University Press, [1980] ©1980; 1980.
26. Mawson C. *Psychoanalysis and Anxiety: From Knowing to Being.* Abingdon: Routledge; 2019.
27. Nietzsche FW. *Beyond good and evil: Prelude to a philosophy of the future.* London; New York: Penguin Books, [1990] ©1990; 1990.
28. Blits JH. Hobbesian Fear. *Political Theory.* 1989;17(3):417–31.
29. Svendsen. *A Philosophy of Fear.*
30. Barlow. Unraveling the mysteries of anxiety; May R. *The Meaning of Anxiety* 1950.
31. Tyrer P. *Anxiety: A Multidisciplinary Review.* London: Imperial College Press, 1999.
32. Ibid.

33. Svendsen. *A Philosophy of Fear.*
34. Ibid.
35. May. *The Meaning of Anxiety.*

CHAPTER 6: FEAR: THE PRIMARY PSYCHOLOGICAL FORCE

1. Freud, S. (1963). Introductory lectures on psycho-analysis: Lecture 25. Anxiety. In Strachey, J, ed. and trans. *The standard edition of the complete psychological works of Sigmund Freud (Vol. 16).* London: Hogarth Press. (Original work published 1917).

2. van der Schaaf ME, Schmidt K, Kaur J, et al. Acquisition learning is stronger for aversive than appetitive events. *Communications Biology.* 2022;5(1):302.

3. Baumeister RF, Bratslavsky E, Finkenauer C, Vohs KD. Bad is stronger than good. *Review of General Psychology.* 2001;5(4):323–70.

4. Marcus GE, MacKuen MB. *Anxiety, Enthusiasm, and the Vote: The Emotional Underpinnings of Learning and Involvement During Presidential Campaigns.* New York: Psychology Press; 2004.

5. Solomon. *The Passions.*

6. Baumeister et al. Bad is stronger than good.

7. Markett S, Montag C, Reuter M. Anxiety and Harm Avoidance. In: Absher JR, Cloutier J, eds. *Neuroimaging Personality, Social Cognition, and Character.* San Diego: Academic Press; 2016:91–112.

8. Adolphs R. The biology of fear. *Curr Biol.* 2013;23(2):R79–93.

9. Bargh JA, Morsella E. The Unconscious Mind. *Perspect Psychol Sci.* 2008;3(1):73-79.

10. Rebughini P. A sociology of anxiety: Western modern legacy and the Covid-19 outbreak. *International Sociology.* 2021;36(4):554–68.

11. Vazard J, Kurth C. Apprehending anxiety: an introduction to the Topical Collection on worry and wellbeing. *Synthese.* 2022;200(4):327.

12. Ibid.; Lormand E. Toward a theory of moods. *Philosophical Studies.* 1985;47(3): 385–407.

13. Mowrer. Two-factor learning theory.

14. Dantzer R. The Psychology of Fear and Stress, J.A. Gray (Ed.). Cambridge University Press, Cambridge (1987), pp. viii and 422. *Behavioural Processes.* 1989;18; Gable SL, Reis HT, Elliot AJ. Behavioral activation and inhibition in everyday life. *Journal of personality and social psychology.* 2000;78 6:1135–49; Gray JA. Précis of The neuropsychology of anxiety: An enquiry into the functions of the septo-hippocampal system. *Behavioral and Brain Sciences.* 1982;5(3):469–84.

15. Bechara et al. Deciding advantageously before knowing the advantageous strategy.

16. Freud, Introductory lectures on psycho-analysis: Lecture 25. Anxiety.

17. Ibid.

CHAPTER 7: BENEFITS OF ANXIETY

1. Adolphs. The biology of fear; Harper CA, Satchell LP, Fido D, Latzman RD. Functional Fear Predicts Public Health Compliance in the COVID-19 Pandemic. *International Journal of Mental Health and Addiction.* 2021;19(5):1875–88.

2. Vazard, Kurth. Apprehending anxiety.

3. van der Schaaf et al. Acquisition learning is stronger for aversive than appetitive events.

4. Ibid.

5. Eysenck MW, Derakshan N, Santos R, Calvo MG. Anxiety and cognitive performance: attentional control theory. *Emotion.* 2007;7(2):336–53.

6. Kurth. Moral Anxiety and Moral Agency; Vazard. Epistemic Anxiety.

7. Vazard. Epistemic Anxiety; Nagel J. Epistemic anxiety and adaptive invariantism. *Philosophical Perspectives.* 2010;24(1):407–35.

8. Mitte. Anxiety and risky decision-making; Hockey GRJ, Maule AJ, Clough PJ, Bdzola L. Effects of negative mood states on risk in everyday decision making. *Cognition and Emotion.* 2000;14(6):823–56.

9. Howlett JR, Paulus MP. Individual Differences in Subjective Utility and Risk Preferences: The Influence of Hedonic Capacity and Trait Anxiety. *Frontiers in psychiatry.* 2017;8:88.

10. Charpentier CJ, Aylward J, Roiser JP, Robinson OJ. Enhanced Risk Aversion, But Not Loss Aversion, in Unmedicated Pathological Anxiety. *Biol Psychiatry.* 2017;81(12):1014–22; Giorgetta C, Grecucci A, Zuanon S, et al. Reduced risk-taking behavior as a trait feature of anxiety. *Emotion.* 2012;12(6):1373–83.

11. Charpentier et al. Enhanced Risk Aversion.

12. Maner JK, Schmidt NB. The role of risk avoidance in anxiety. *Behavior Therapy.* 2006;37(2):181–89.

13. Strack J, Esteves F. Exams? Why worry? Interpreting anxiety as facilitative and stress appraisals. *Anxiety Stress Coping.* 2015;28(2):205–14.

14. Lukasik KM, Waris O, Soveri A, Lehtonen M, Laine M. The Relationship of Anxiety and Stress with Working Memory Performance in a Large Non-depressed Sample. *Frontiers in Psychology.* 2019;10.

15. Strack, Esteves. Exams? Why worry?

16. Drach-Zahavy A, Erez M. Challenge versus threat effects on the goal-performance relationship. *Organizational Behavior and Human Decision Processes.* 2002;88(2):667–82.

17. Davis M, Walker DL, Miles L, Grillon C. Phasic vs Sustained Fear in Rats and Humans: Role of the Extended Amygdala in Fear vs Anxiety. *Neuropsychopharmacology.* 2010;35(1):105–35.

18. Strack J, Lopes P, Esteves F, Fernandez-Berrocal P. Must We Suffer to Succeed? *Journal of Individual Differences.* 2017;38(2):113–24.

19. Izard C, Ackerman B. *Motivational, Organizational and Regulatory Functions of Discrete Emotions. Handbook of Emotions.* New York: Guilford Press; 2000.

20. Yerkes RM, Dodson JD. The relation of strength of stimulus to rapidity of habit-formation. *Journal of Comparative Neurology & Psychology.* 1908;18:459–82.

21. Diamond DM, Campbell AM, Park CR, Halonen J, Zoladz PR. The temporal dynamics model of emotional memory processing: a synthesis on the neurobiological basis of stress-induced amnesia, flashbulb and traumatic memories, and the Yerkes-Dodson law. *Neural Plast.* 2007:60803.

22. Broadhurst PL. Emotionality and the Yerkes-Dodson Law. *Journal of Experimental Psychology.* 1957;54(5):345–52; Dickman SJ. Dimensions of arousal: Wakefulness and vigor. *Human Factors.* 2002;44(3):429–42.

23. Lewis RS, Nikolova A, Chang DJ, Weekes NY. Examination stress and components of working memory. *Stress: The International Journal on the Biology of Stress.* 2008;11(2):108–14.

24. Seipp B. Anxiety and academic performance: A meta-analysis of findings. *Anxiety Stress and Coping–ANXIETY STRESS COPING.* 1991;4:27–41.

25. Sandi C. Stress and cognition. *WIREs Cognitive Science.* 2013;4(3):245–61.

26. Ibid.

27. Potvin O, Bergua V, Meillon C, et al. State anxiety and cognitive functioning in older adults. *The American Journal of Geriatric Psychiatry.* 2013;21(9):915–24.

28. Eysenck, MW, Calvo, MG. Anxiety and performance: The processing efficiency theory. *Cognition and Emotion,* 1992;6(6): 409–34.

29. Tanaka M, Yoshida M, Emoto H, Ishii H. Noradrenaline systems in the hypothalamus, amygdala and locus coeruleus are involved in the provocation of anxiety: basic studies. *Eur J Pharmacol.* 2000;405(1–3):397–406.

30. Hämmerer D, Callaghan MF, Hopkins A, et al. Locus coeruleus integrity in old age is selectively related to memories linked with salient negative events. *Proceedings of the National Academy of Sciences.* 2018;115(9):2228–33.

31. Park J, Moghaddam B. Impact of anxiety on prefrontal cortex encoding of cognitive flexibility. *Neuroscience.* 2017;345:193–202.

32. Coplan et al. The relationship between intelligence and anxiety; Penney A, Miedema V, Mazmanian D. Intelligence and emotional disorders: Is the worrying and ruminating mind a more intelligent mind? *Personality and Individual Differences.* 2015; 74:90–93.

33. Ibid.

34. Perkins AM, Corr PJ. Can worriers be winners? The association between worrying and job performance. *Personality and Individual Differences.* 2005;38(1):25–31.

35. Ibid.

36. Coplan et al. The relationship between intelligence and anxiety.

37. Penney, Miedema, Mazmanian. Intelligence and emotional disorders.

38. MacKuen M, Wolak J, Keele L, Marcus G. Civic engagements: Resolute partisanship or reflective deliberation. *American Journal of Political Science.* 2010;54:440–58.

39. Tiedens LZ, Linton S. Judgment under emotional certainty and uncertainty: The effects of specific emotions on information processing. *J Pers Soc Psychol.* 2001;81(6): 973–88.

40. Messer S. The effect of anxiety over intellectual performance on reflection-impulsivity in children. *Child Development.* 1970;41(3):723–35.

41. Salovey P, Mayer JD, Goldman SL, Turvey C, Palfai TP. Emotional attention, clarity, and repair: Exploring emotional intelligence using the Trait Meta-Mood Scale. In: *Emotion, Disclosure, & Health.* Washington, DC: American Psychological Association; 1995:125–54.

42. Strack et al. Must we suffer to succeed?

43. Dillard JP, Plotnick CA, Godbold LC, Freimuth VS, Edgar T. The multiple affective outcomes of AIDS PSAs: Fear appeals do more than scare people. *Communication Research*. 1996;23(1):44–72; Maddux JE, Rogers RW. Protection motivation and self-efficacy: A revised theory of fear appeals and attitude change. *Journal of Experimental Social Psychology*. 1983;19(5):469–79.

44. Leventhal H, Watts JC, Pagano F. Effects of fear and instructions on how to cope with danger. *Journal of Personality and Social Psychology*. 1967;6(3):313–21.

45. Tannenbaum et al. Appealing to fear.

46. de Hoog N, Stroebe W, Wit J. The impact of vulnerability to and severity of a health risk on processing and acceptance of fear-arousing communications: A meta-analysis. *Review of General Psychology*. 2007;11.

47. Tannenbaum et al. Appealing to fear.

48. Pier KS. Disulfiram and acamprosate. In Boland, R, Verduin, ML, eds. Kaplan & Sadock's *Comprehensive Textbook of Psychiatry*. Philadelphia: Wolters Kluwer; 2025, 3369.

49. Colder CR, Scalco M, Trucco EM, et al. Prospective associations of internalizing and externalizing problems and their co-occurrence with early adolescent substance use. *J Abnorm Child Psychol*. 2013;41(4):667–77; McCauley Ohannessian C. Anxiety and substance use during adolescence. *Subst Abus*. 2014;35(4):418–25.

50. Hengen KM, Alpers GW. Stress makes the difference: Social stress and social anxiety in decision-making under uncertainty. *Frontiers in Psychology*. 2021;12.

51. Cohen-Chen S, Halperin E, Porat R, Bar-Tal D. The differential effects of hope and fear on information processing in intractable conflict. *Journal of Social and Political Psychology*. 2014;2(1):11–30; Huang TY, Souitaris V, Barsade SG. Which matters more? Group fear versus hope in entrepreneurial escalation of commitment. *Strategic Management Journal*. 2019;40(11):1852–81.

52. Tannenbaum et al. Appealing to fear.

53. Eysenck. *Anxiety*; Gladstone G, Parker G. What's the use of worrying? Its function and its dysfunction. *Aust N Z J Psychiatry*. 2003;37(3):347–54.

54. Hendrickx L, Vlek C, Oppewal H. Relative importance of scenario information and frequency information in the judgment of risk. *Acta Psychologica*. 1989;72(1):41–63.

55. Weinstein ND. Effects of personal experience on self-protective behavior. *Psychological Bulletin*. 1989;105(1):31–50.

56. Cloninger & Svrakic. In Kaplan and Saddock *Comprehensive textbook of psychiatry*. 2017.

57. Giorgetta et al. Reduced risk-taking behavior as a trait feature of anxiety.

58. Maner, Schmidt. The role of risk avoidance in anxiety; Broman-Fulks JJ, Urbaniak A, Bondy CL, Toomey KJ. Anxiety sensitivity and risk-taking behavior. *Anxiety, Stress & Coping: An International Journal*. 2014;27(6):619–32.

59. Mitte K. Anxiety and risky decision-making: The role of subjective probability and subjective costs of negative events. *Personality and Individual Differences*. 2007;43:243–53.

60. Smith, Ebert, Broman-Fulks. The relationship between anxiety and risk taking is moderated by ambiguity.

61. Wohl MJA, Branscombe NR. Collective angst: How threats to the future vitality of the ingroup shape intergroup emotion. In: *Transcending Self-Interest: Psychological*

Explorations of the Quiet Ego. Washington, DC: American Psychological Association; 2008:171–81.

62. Marcus GE, MacKuen MB. Anxiety, enthusiasm, and the vote: The emotional underpinnings of learning and involvement during presidential campaigns. *American Political Science Review.* 1993;87(3):672–85.

CHAPTER 8: ROLE OF FEAR IN HUMAN LIFE AND IN CIVIL SOCIETY: CONSEQUENCES OF FEARLESSNESS

1. Liddell, H. S. (1949). The role of vigilance in the development of animal neurosis. In P. Hoch J. Zub (eds.), *Anxiety.* New York: Grune Stratton.

2. Kurth C. Anxiety, normative uncertainty, and social regulation. *Biology & Philosophy.* 2016;31.

3. Luu et al. Anxiety and the motivational basis of working memory.

4. Barrash J, Stuss DT, Aksan N, et al. "Frontal lobe syndrome"? Subtypes of acquired personality disturbances in patients with focal brain damage. *Cortex.* 2018;106:65–80.

5. Loewenstein G, Schwartz D. *Nothing to Fear but a Lack of Fear: Climate Change and the Fear Deficit.* 2017.

6. Clarke L. Risk society: Towards a new modernity. *Social Forces.* 1994;73:328+.

7. Tiedens, Linton. Judgment under emotional certainty and uncertainty.

8. Twenge JM. The age of anxiety? Birth cohort change in anxiety and neuroticism, 1952-1993. *J Pers Soc Psychol.* 2000;79(6):1007–21; Schürmann J, Margraf J. Age of anxiety and depression revisited: A meta-analysis of two European community samples (1964–2015). *International Journal of Clinical and Health Psychology.* 2018;18(2):102–12.

9. Jackson, Everts. Anxiety as social practice.

10. Brennan T. *The Transmission of Affect.* Ithaca, NY: Cornell University Press; 2004.

11. Blair RJ, Peschardt KS, Budhani S, Mitchell DG, Pine DS. The development of psychopathy. *J Child Psychol Psychiatry.* 2006;47(3–4):262–76.

12. Kochanska G. Multiple pathways to conscience for children with different temperaments: From toddlerhood to age 5. *Dev Psychol.* 1997;33(2):228–40.

13. Waller R, Shaw DS, Hyde LW. Observed fearlessness and positive parenting interact to predict childhood callous-unemotional behaviors among low-income boys. *J Child Psychol Psychiatry.* 2017;58(3):282–91.

14. Hare RD, Frazelle J, Cox DN. Psychopathy and physiological responses to threat of an aversive stimulus. *Psychophysiology.* 1978;15(2):165–72; Newman JP, Curtin JJ, Bertsch JD, Baskin-Sommers AR. Attention moderates the fearlessness of psychopathic offenders. *Biol Psychiatry.* 2010;67(1):66–70; Birbaumer N, Veit R, Lotze M, et al. Deficient fear conditioning in psychopathy: A functional magnetic resonance imaging study. *Archives of General Psychiatry.* 2005;62(7):799–805.

15. Cleckley HM. *The Mask of Sanity: An Attempt to Clarify Some Issues About the So-Called Psychopathic Personality.* Martino Publishing. 2015.

16. Loewenstein G, Weber E, Hsee C, Welch N. Risk as feelings. *Psychological bulletin.* 2001;127:267–86.

17. Satchell LP, Bacon AM, Firth JL, Corr PJ. Risk as reward: Reinforcement sensitivity theory and psychopathic personality perspectives on everyday risk-taking. *Personality and Individual Differences.* 2018;128:162–69.

18. Gao Y, Raine A, Venables PH, Dawson ME, Mednick SA. Association of poor childhood fear conditioning and adult crime. *Am J Psychiatry.* 2010;167(1):56–60.

19. Raine A, Reynolds C, Venables PH, Mednick SA, Farrington DP. Fearlessness, stimulation-seeking, and large body size at age 3 years as early predispositions to childhood aggression at age 11 years. *Archives of General Psychiatry.* 1998;55(8):745–51.

20. Hoppenbrouwers SS, Bulten BH, Brazil IA. Parsing fear: A reassessment of the evidence for fear deficits in psychopathy. *Psychol Bull.* 2016;142(6):573–600.

21. Anderson NE, Widdows M, Maurer JM, Kiehl KA. Clarifying fearlessness in psychopathy: An examination of thrill-seeking and physical risk-taking. *J Psychopathol Behav Assess.* 2021;43(1):21–32.

22. LeDoux JE. Coming to terms with fear. *Proc Natl Acad Sci U S A.* 2014;111(8): 2871–78.

23. Birbaumer et al. Deficient fear conditioning in psychopathy; Schultz DH, Balderston NL, Baskin-Sommers AR, Larson CL, Helmstetter FJ. Psychopaths show enhanced amygdala activation during fear conditioning. *Frontiers in Psychology.* 2016;7.

24. Johanson M, Vaurio O, Tiihonen J, Lähteenvuo M. A Systematic Literature Review of Neuroimaging of Psychopathic Traits. *Frontiers in Psychiatry.* 2020;10; Thomson ND, Aboutanos M, Kiehl KA, Neumann C, Galusha C, Fanti KA. Physiological reactivity in response to a fear-induced virtual reality experience: Associations with psychopathic traits. *Psychophysiology.* 2019;56(1):e13276; Yang Y, Raine A, Narr KL, Colletti P, Toga AW. Localization of deformations within the amygdala in individuals with psychopathy. *Archives of General Psychiatry.* 2009;66(9):986–94.

25. Lamoureux VA, Glenn AL. An analysis of conscious fear and automatic threat response in psychopathy. *Personal Disord.* 2021;12(2):171–81.

26. Pardini DA, Raine A, Erickson K, Loeber R. Lower amygdala volume in men is associated with childhood aggression, early psychopathic traits, and future violence. *Biol Psychiatry.* 2014;75(1):73–80.

27. Hofmann MJ, Schneider S, Mokros A. Fearless but anxious? A systematic review on the utility of fear and anxiety levels to classify subtypes of psychopathy. *Behavioral Sciences & the Law.* 2021;39(5):512–40.

28. Karpman B. On the need of separating psychopathy into two distinct clinical types: the symptomatic and the idiopathic. *Journal of Criminal Psychopathology.* 1941;3:112–37.

29. Hare RD, Neumann CS. Structural models of psychopathy. *Curr Psychiatry Rep.* 2005;7(1):57–64.

30. Hofmann, Schneider, Mokros. Fearless but anxious?

31. Grillon C. Startle reactivity and anxiety disorders: aversive conditioning, context, and neurobiology. *Biol Psychiatry.* 2002;52(10):958–75.

32. Fowles DC. Electrodermal hyporeactivity and antisocial behavior: does anxiety mediate the relationship? *J Affect Disord.* 2000;61(3):177–89.

33. Sacco, V. (2005), *When Crime Waves.* Thousand Oaks, CA: Sage Publications/Pine Forge Press.

34. Englot DJ, Morgan VL, Chang C. Impaired vigilance networks in temporal lobe epilepsy: Mechanisms and clinical implications. *Epilepsia.* 2020;61(2):189–202.

35. Zuckerman M. *Behavioral Expressions and Biosocial Bases of Sensation Seeking.* New York: Cambridge University Press; 1994.

36. Knowles KA, Olatunji BO. Anxiety and safety behavior usage during the COVID-19 pandemic: The prospective role of contamination fear. *J Anxiety Disord.* 2021; 77:102323.

37. Kurth. Moral anxiety and moral agency; Vazard, Kurth. Apprehending anxiety.

38. Koleva S, Selterman D, Iyer R, Ditto P, Graham J. The moral compass of insecurity: Anxious and avoidant attachment predict moral judgment. *Social Psychological and Personality Science.* 2013;5(2):185–94.

39. Gladstone, Parker. What's the use of worrying?

40. Tallis F, Davey GCL, Capuzzo N. The phenomenology of non-pathological worry: A preliminary investigation. In: *Worrying: Perspectives on Theory, Assessment and Treatment.* Oxford, England: John Wiley & Sons; 1994:61–89.

41. Gladstone, Parker. What's the use of worrying?

42. Liska AE, Warner BD. Functions of crime: A paradoxical process. *American Journal of Sociology.* 1991;96(6):1441–63.

43. Jackson J, Gray E. Functional fear and public insecurities about crime. *British Journal of Criminology.* 2010;50.

44. Ibid.

45. Schwartz SH, Bardi A. Value hierarchies across cultures: Taking a similarities perspective. *Journal of Cross-Cultural Psychology.* 2001;32(3):268–90.

46. Schwartz S. An overview of the Schwartz theory of basic values. *Online Readings in Psychology and Culture.* 2012;2.

47. Maslow AH. *Toward a Psychology of Being.* New York: D. Van Nostrand Company; 1968; Baumeister RF, Leary MR. The need to belong: Desire for interpersonal attachments as a fundamental human motivation. *Psychological bulletin.* 1995;117 3:497–529.

48. Bowlby. Attachment and loss; Leary MR. Responses to social exclusion: Social anxiety, jealousy, loneliness, depression, and low self-esteem. *Journal of Social and Clinical Psychology.* 1990;9(2):221–29.

49. Craighead WE, Kimball WH, Rehak PJ. Mood changes, physiological responses, and self-statements during social rejection imagery. *J Consult Clin Psychol.* 1979;47(2):385–96; Horney K. *Our inner conflicts, a constructive theory of neurosis.* New York: W.W. Norton & Company, Inc.; 1945.

50. Jordan J, Mullen E, Murnighan JK. Striving for the Moral Self: The effects of recalling past moral actions on future moral behavior. *Personality and Social Psychology Bulletin.* 2011;37(5):701–13.

51. Ibid.

52. Ibid.; Gilbert P. The relationship of shame, social anxiety and depression: the role of the evaluation of social rank. *Clinical Psychology & Psychotherapy.* 2000;7(3):174–89.

53. Bechara et al. Deciding advantageously before knowing the advantageous strategy.

54. Loewenstein et al. Risk as feelings.
55. Sacco, V. *When Crime Waves.*
56. Koleva S, Selterman D, Iyer R, Ditto P, Graham J. The moral compass of insecurity: Anxious and avoidant attachment predict moral judgment. *Social Psychological and Personality Science.* 2014;5:185–94.
57. Ibid.
58. Robinson JS, Joel S, Plaks JE. Empathy for the group versus indifference toward the victim: Effects of anxious and avoidant attachment on moral judgment. *Journal of Experimental Social Psychology.* 2015;56:139–52.
59. Ibid.
60. Feeney JA, Noller P. Attachment style as a predictor of adult romantic relationships. *Journal of Personality and Social Psychology.* 1990;58:281–91; Rom E, Mikulincer M. Attachment theory and group processes: The association between attachment style and group-related representations, goals, memories, and functioning. *Journal of Personality and Social Psychology.* 2003;84:1220–35.
61. Impett EA, Peplau LA. Why some women consent to unwanted sex with a dating partner: Insights from attachment theory. *Psychology of Women Quarterly.* 2002;26(4):360–70.
62. Gillath O, Shaver PR, Mikulincer M, Nitzberg RE, Erez A, Van Ijzendoorn MH. Attachment, caregiving, and volunteering: Placing volunteerism in an attachment-theoretical framework. *Personal Relationships.* 2005;12:425–46.
63. Kogut T, Kogut E. Exploring the relationship between adult attachment style and the identifiable victim effect in helping behavior. *Journal of Experimental Social Psychology.* 2013;49:651–60.
64. Feeney, Collins. Predictors of caregiving in adult intimate relationships.
65. Simpson et al. Attachment and the management of empathic accuracy in relationship-threatening situations.
66. Ibid.
67. Bartz J, Lydon J. Relationship-specific attachment, risk regulation, and communal norm adherence in close relationships. *Journal of Experimental Social Psychology.* 2008;44:655–63.
68. Gineikiene J, Fennis BM, Barauskaite D, van Koningsbruggen GM. Stress can help or hinder novelty seeking: The role of consumer life history strategies. *International Journal of Research in Marketing.* 2022;39(4):1042–58.
69. Burkhardt BR, Schwarz RM, Green SB. Relationships between dimensions of anxiety and sensation seeking. *Journal of Consulting and Clinical Psychology.* 1978;46:194–95.
70. Kampman O, Viikki M, Järventausta K, Leinonen E. Meta-analysis of anxiety disorders and temperament. *Neuropsychobiology.* 2014;69(3):175–86.
71. Arnett JJ. Sensation seeking, aggressiveness, and adolescent reckless behavior. *Personality and Individual Differences.* 1996;20:693–702; Zuckerman M. *Sensation Seeking and Risky Behavior.* Washington, DC: American Psychological Association; 2007.
72. Marcus, MacKuen. *Anxiety, Enthusiasm, and the Vote.*

Notes

Chapter 9: Optimal Anxiety

1. Loewenstein et al. Risk as feelings.
2. Foa et al. Cognitive biases in generalized social phobia; Mitte. Anxiety and risky decision-making.
3. Stöber. Trait anxiety and pessimistic appraisal of risk and chance; Mitte. Anxiety and risky decision-making.
4. Penney et al. Intelligence and emotional disorders.
5. Marks, Nesse. Fear and fitness.
6. Talebi Rezaabadi O. The relationships between social class anxiety, facilitative anxiety and reading test performance. *Southern African Linguistics and Applied Language Studies*. 2017;35:211–23; Hollandsworth JG, Glazeski RC, Kirkland K, Jones GE, Van Norman LR. An analysis of the nature and effects of test anxiety: Cognitive, behavioral, and physiological components. *Cognitive Therapy and Research*. 1979;3(2):165–80; Kader A. Debilitating and facilitating test anxiety and student motivation and achievement in principles of microeconomics. *International Review of Economics Education*. 2016;23.
7. Hollandsworth et al. An analysis of the nature and effects of test anxiety.
8. Welesilassie MW, Nikolov M. Relationships between motivation and anxiety in adult EFL learners at an Ethiopian university. *Ampersand*. 2022;9:100089; Cunningham GB, Ashley FB. Debilitative and facilitative perceptions of trait anxiety among students in a college golf class. *Percept Mot Skills*. 2002;94(3 Pt 1):739–42.
9. Alpert R, Haber RN. Anxiety in academic achievement situations. *The Journal of Abnormal and Social Psychology*. 1960;61:207–15; Kestenbaum JM, Weiner B. Achievement performance related to achievement motivation and text anxiety. *Journal of Consulting and Clinical Psychology*. 1970;34:343–44; Deffenbacher JL. Worry, emotionality, and task-generated interference in test anxiety: An empirical test of attentional theory. *Journal of Educational Psychology*. 1978;70:248–54.
10. Ibid.; Smith RE, Ascough JC, Ettinger RF, Nelson DA. Humor, anxiety, and task performance. *Journal of Personality and Social Psychology*. 1971;19:243–46.
11. Deffenbacher. Worry, emotionality, and task-generated interference in test anxiety.
12. Smith et al. Humor, anxiety, and task performance.
13. Deffenbacher. Worry, emotionality, and task-generated interference in test anxiety.
14. Ibid.
15. Ibid.; Vos T, Flaxman AD, Naghavi M, et al. Years lived with disability (YLDs) for 1160 sequelae of 289 diseases and injuries 1990–2010: a systematic analysis for the Global Burden of Disease Study 2010. *Lancet*. 2012;380(9859):2163–96.
16. Loewenstein et al. Risk as feelings.
17. Zajonc RB. Feeling and thinking: Preferences need no inferences. *American Psychologist*. 1980;35:151–75.
18. Leventhal H, Watts JC. Sources of resistance to fear-arousing communications on smoking and lung cancer. *Journal of Personality*. 1966;34(2):155–75.

Chapter Ten: Conclusions

1. de Cervantes, Miguel. *Don Quixote*.